W9-BRP-431

LEADING FOR POWERFUL LEARNING

LEADING FOR POWERFUL LEARNING

A Guide for Instructional Leaders

Angela Breidenstein
Kevin Fahey
Carl Glickman
Frances Hensley

Teachers College
Columbia University
New York and London

Published by Teachers College Press, 1234 Amsterdam Avenue, New York, NY 10027

The authors would like to express gratitude for permission to use the following:

Figure 4.2, from *Teaching as Inquiry: Asking Hard Questions to Improve Practice and
Student Achievement*, by A. Weinbaum, D. Allen, T. Blythe, K. Simon, S. Seidel, and C.
Rubin, 2004, New York, Teachers College Press. Used with permission from Steve Seidel at
Project Zero.

Appendix A, from "Wondering to Be Done: The Collaborative Assessment Conference," by
S. Seidel, in D. Allen (Ed.), *Assessing Student Learning: From Grading to Understanding*
(pp. 21–39), 1998, New York, Teachers College Press. Used with permission.

Appendix B: The *Tuning* protocol originally was developed by Joseph McDonald and the
Coalition of Essential Schools Exhibitions Project. The protocol was further developed
by David Allen, which is the version included here and used with permission from David
Allen (*Assessing Student Learning: From Grading to Understanding,* by D. Allen (Ed.),
1998, New York, Teachers College Press).

Appendix C: The *Consultancy* protocol is used with permission from Paula Evans, Gene
Thompson-Grove, and the School Reform Initiative.

Appendix D: Establishing Ground Rules, is used with permission from Marylyn Wentworth
and the School Reform Initiative.

The authors also wish to acknowledge the following:

Appendix E: "Setting Norms for Collaborative Work," n.d., was retrieved from http://www.
scoe.org/files/setting-norms.pdf

Library of Congress Cataloging-in-Publication Data

Leading for powerful learning : a guide for instructional leaders / Angela Breidenstein ... [et al.].
   p. cm.
  Includes bibliographical references and index.
  ISBN 978-0-8077-5349-1 (pbk. : alk. paper)
  1. School supervision—United States. 2. Educational leadership—United States. 3. Teacher
effectiveness—United States. 4. Effective teaching—United States. I. Breidenstein, Angela.
  LB2806.4.L43 2012
  371.2'03—dc23

                2012020750

ISBN 978-0-8077-5349-1 (paperback)

Printed on acid-free paper
Manufactured in the United States of America

19 18 17 16 15 14 13 12   8 7 6 5 4 3 2 1

Contents

Prologue

I'm honored that my colleagues Angela Breidenstein, Kevin Fahey, and Frances Hensley included me in creating a book far better than what I could have done alone. In the early 1980s, I wrote my first books about school leadership, supervision, and school improvement based on experiences as a school principal in New England and later as a professor working with K–12 schools throughout the southeast. I used my understanding of adult and group development for school leaders to differentiate approaches to help teachers, individually and collectively, to grow in knowledge, wisdom, and craft.

And now, nearly 30 years later, my co-authors have a lens on school practices and leadership grounded in my original work but far more current and comprehensive. The central thesis is that school improvement is adult learning. For students to learn well, adults themselves need to be persistent learners. *Leading for Powerful Learning* is about the most powerful ways to practice instructional leadership. The role of an instructional leader is to challenge all adults, including learning in new, developmental, and, sometimes, uncomfortable ways. The book conceptualizes comprehensive stages of teacher and school development, and matches these stages with ways to select and use the methods of coaching, critical friends groups, learning communities, inquiring into practice, mentoring, and clinical and nondirective supervision, to name only a few.

Working to improve our schools is a wonderful way to spend a career. I feel fortunate to have worked at this long enough to see my ideas about improving education transformed by Angela, Kevin, and Frances into practical elegance rooted in the real world of schools today.

Carl Glickman

Acknowledgments

Whatever "heart" this book possesses, is due in large measure to the participation and wisdom of the instructional leaders whose voices are heard throughout its pages. We thank Kathy Bieser, Michael Cardona, Rubén Carmona, Wayne Clark, Suzanne Charochak, Jennifer Flewelling, Matt Fusco, Addie Hawkins, Ileana Liberatore, Annie Leonard, Doug Lyons, Julie MacDonald, Elizabeth Mathews, Mindy Paulo, Cathy O'Connell, Jeff Price, Susan Snyder, Gene Thompson-Grove, Justin Vernon, and Kelley Young. We also want to acknowledge those whose real names we did not use so that they could share freely both the challenges and rewards of this work, and thank the many other colleagues who contributed to our thinking and this book's development. In addition, we are in debt to Shari Albright, Gene Thompson-Grove, and Thomas Van Soelen for their initial reading of our manuscript and for the thoughtfulness and common sense that characterized their feedback. We are grateful to David Allen, Paula Evans, Steve Seidel, Gene Thompson-Grove, and Marylyn Wentworth for allowing us to include their work.

We also want to acknowledge a variety of institutions that have supported this work. Deep appreciation extends to Salem State University, Trinity University, and the University of Georgia for their continuing support for our professional lives. Thanks to the School Reform Initiative located in Denver, Colorado, for providing a laboratory in which many, if not all, of the ideas in this book have been piloted, tested, and improved. Finally, thanks to the editorial team at Teachers College Press for its sound advice, faith in our work, and kindness to our geographically sprawling but like-minded writing team.

LEADING FOR POWERFUL LEARNING

CHAPTER 1

Why Leadership for
Adult Learning Is Crucial

It is not hard to imagine this scenario. It is 30 minutes before school starts for the day. Teachers are walking toward their rooms, chatting about the weather, their own children, the local news, or the traffic. Some are speculating about this weekend's high school football game, others wondering about possible budget cuts or next week's field trip. Some stop to say good morning to old friends, others check in with the teacher in the next room. There's a lot to talk about.

Before long, a bell rings and students swarm into the halls, banging lockers, getting books, chatting with friends, and waiting until the last minute to enter their classroom. As quickly as the noise began, it ends. The doors to the classrooms close and the day begins. As you imagine this typical school scene you also might wonder: But what goes on behind those closed doors? What is happening between students and teachers? How is what is occurring in one classroom connected to what is taking place in other classrooms?

It is also not hard to imagine that behind these closed doors the teachers have a variety of experience, expertise, and interests, and are at very different stages of their careers. In our imagined hall in our imagined school, there might be teachers fresh out of a graduate program who are knowledgeable about the district's standards-based social studies curriculum but have a tough time getting their students to the cafeteria without disrupting other classes. Across from them there might be a teacher who is wonderful at helping most students become better writers but struggles with students who speak another language at home. Next to him might be a veteran who is a brilliant math teacher, but is challenged by the district's new emphasis on writing across the curriculum. At the very end of the hall might be two experienced teachers—both former special education teachers—who are very skilled practitioners, but who worry whether their professional practice is serving the needs of students of color who are leaving school at increasingly high rates. So what do these very different teachers have in common? They all have something to learn.

Schools are complex places and teachers are complicated people. Yet in our imaginary hallway in our imaginary school, every teacher has something to learn. The new teacher needs to learn about classroom management, the brilliant writing teacher needs to learn about working with second language students, and the talented math teacher needs to learn about supporting content-area writing. The veteran teachers want to learn about the connections between their practice and the students of color who never finish school. Teachers need (and want) to learn.

TEACHERS AS LEARNERS

Our scenario suggests not only that teachers need to be learners, but also that much of the learning they need, can be found in their own school or hallway. The new teacher might learn a lot about classroom management from the brilliant math teacher. The brilliant math teacher might learn about writing in content areas from the recent grads who are steeped in the latest research and current literacy practice. The successful writing teacher might learn about helping second language students from the teacher who is a former special education teacher. The two most senior teachers might learn about the connection between the school's teaching practice and the increasing district dropout rates by talking to teachers who graduated from the district's schools.

In most schools, there are teachers who are gifted math teachers or who work well with diverse populations or who understand how to engage reluctant learners, yet because the doors in schools typically are closed, the knowledge teachers possess often is lost. Because teachers work in isolation, and because their conversations frequently are limited to unstructured talk about sports, their children, budgets, the weather, and the traffic, the practice-related knowledge that exists in schools is not always communicated. The teacher who struggles with using the district's new math program might

There is no other way than collaboration, collegiality, and collective responsibility. This is what we do. We look at our practice and we figure out how to make it better. Because you know what? You don't have it all figured out.

—Jennifer Flewelling, Principal,
North Beverly Elementary School,
Beverly, Massachusetts

work in the same hall as a teacher who has a deep understanding of the program, but the struggling teacher never has a chance to access his colleague's expertise. The accomplished science teacher who is concerned about her students' ability to read text may never interact with the former special education teacher who understands adolescent literacy. Sadly, schools are often places full of powerful learning, great expertise, and good practice that are not taken advantage of—and that affects students.

How do schools become better places for kids? The answer is not so complicated. Schools become better places for kids when teachers become better teachers, when they relentlessly improve their practice, when they are learners. Moreover, teachers (or any other educators, for that matter) cannot improve their craft in isolation from others. How do teachers improve their practice if they receive no feedback from students or colleagues, if they never observe other adults teach, if other adults never watch them teach, if teachers never look at students' work with colleagues, or if they never struggle to understand complex pedagogical practices with others?

We have now a substantial professional knowledge base that highlights a strong connection between student and adult learning. Student learning increases in schools where there are educator communities that are reflective, collaborative, and focused on issues of teaching and learning (Bryk, Sebring, Allensworth, Luppescu, & Easton, 2010; Donaldson, 2008; Guskey, 2000; Leithwood, Louis, Anderson, & Wahlstrom, 2004; Stoll & Louis, 2007). When adults learn from one another, student learning increases. Adult learning makes a difference.

More specifically, the literature also suggests that adult learning in schools is best supported when teachers, principals, and superintendents regularly engage in meaningful dialogue with colleagues about improving their practice (Guskey, 1995; Hoffmann & Johnston, 2005; Johnson & the Next Generation of Teachers Project, 2004; Kegan & Lahey, 2009;

> Are kids learning or are we just teaching? You have to create that culture where you can have conversations around instruction. It is far better for us to sit in a meeting and peel the onion about a kid's learning problem than to talk about how we don't have the right books or complain about the parents in the building or about how kids don't do homework. That is so gone now.
>
> —Sue Charochak, Principal,
> Ayers Ryal Side Elementary School,
> Beverly, Massachusetts

McLaughlin & Talbert, 2006; Teitel, 2006). The adult learning that supports improved practice and student achievement often does not happen when adults work in isolation.

INSTRUCTIONAL LEADERSHIP

Despite the hope that the research around the relationship between teacher and student learning holds out for school improvement, the literature also suggests that collaborative, practice-focused, adult learning is not common (Lieberman & Miller, 2008; Schmoker, 2006; Wagner, 2004; Wagner & Kegan, 2006). Hargreaves and Shirley (2009), for example, suggest that schools are still characterized by the isolationism, conservatism, and presentism that Lortie originally described in 1975. The literature on the context of teaching describes how teachers often work by themselves, on only the most pressing, immediate problems, and in ways that reinforce how they have always done things. Learning about practice often gets pushed aside by parent phone calls, paperwork that needs to be filled out, tomorrow's lesson plans, or field trip planning. For lots of very good reasons, sustaining adult learning is not a focus in many schools. Moreover, adults in schools often do not necessarily have the knowledge, expertise, experience, or opportunity to build such learning-focused professional communities. Teacher learning just doesn't happen on its own. It takes leadership.

The leadership that it takes to encourage more learning about practice can be either formal or informal. Certainly principals and superintendents need to be instructional leaders who work tirelessly to create the conditions that support teachers' examining, reflecting on, and improving their practice (Marzano, Waters, & McNulty, 2005; Mitgang & Maeroff, 2008; Waters & Cameron, 2007). However, less formal leaders—department heads, curriculum coaches, mentors, and teachers themselves—play an essential role in this work (Lieberman & Friedrich, 2010; Spillane, 2005). Successful schools understand that the direct improvement of teaching and learning in every classroom comes via a constellation of instructional leaders who undertake a myriad of activities and initiatives that have one goal: improving teaching and learning.

PRACTITIONER LEARNING

Teachers easily accept the idea that children learn in a variety of ways. They also know that as children learn, how they learn also changes. Over time, our students become more abstract, more complex thinkers; they move from struggling with the meaning of a specific word to considering abstract concepts and constructing meaning in a variety of complicated ways. Teachers understand that their students' learning is developmental, and that effectively supporting that learning should take into account the many ways students know and learn. The complex, developmental nature of learning is an idea that is accepted easily when educators think about their students, but just as easily overlooked when they think about what they themselves need to learn in order to improve their professional practice.

CONSTRUCTIVE-DEVELOPMENTAL THEORY

One way of understanding the intricate ways that adult know and learn is by using constructive-developmental theory of adult development (Kegan, 1998). Constructive-developmental theory suggests that much of what we already know about student learning is also relevant to adult learning. The two fundamental premises upon which the theory rests are: (1) adults continually work to make sense of their experiences and (2) the ways that adults make sense of their world can change and grow more complex over time. In a school, this means that adults, depending on a variety of factors, will understand their experiences in very different ways.

A teacher who is worried about lining up his kids for lunch without any disruptive behavior—never mind doing his very best for the second language, gifted, special education, minority, privileged, and so on, kids in his class—is very likely to understand his practice very differently from the master teacher who has an established repertoire and is wondering about how a specific aspect of her literacy practice might be improved. Some teachers can be eager for a right answer to hold on to, while other teachers might resist a prescriptive answer and be more comfortable with an inquiry-like stance toward improving their practice.

While there is no strict timetable for adult development, Kegan does suggest that there are some identifiable stages that leaders interested in supporting teacher development might take into account (Drago-Severson, 2009; Kegan, 1998). However, he also suggests that these stages move along a complex path of adult learning, and that adults move along that path in a variety of ways. Constructive-developmental theory calls the three ways of knowing that are most typical in adults instrumental, socializing, and self-authoring (see Table 1.1 for a summary).

Instrumental Knowers

Instrumental knowers are drawn to specific answers and concrete processes. The teacher struggling with lining up his kids for lunch wants a clear procedure. He wants some concrete steps and specific advice about how to

Table 1.1. Ways of Knowing

Instrumental Knowers	Socializing Knowers	Self-Authoring Knowers
• have concrete needs • believe that rules are important and search for the "right way" • are most comfortable with concrete, specific processes • have limited interest in reflection or collaboration when their own needs are not met	• focus on others • believe that group needs are important • can put a group's needs before their own • can be collaborative and reflective • are uncomfortable with conflicting opinions, values, and behaviors	• are reflective about themselves and their context • can live with ambiguity • evaluate their own actions according to internal standards; expect and accept conflict • consider their personal goals and ideas very important • are able to stand in opposition to a group

get kids to the lunchroom. "Instrumental knowers orient toward following rules and feel supported when others provide specific advice and explicit procedures so that they can accomplish their goals" (Drago-Severson, 2008, p. 61). The opinions and perspectives of others are important to instrumental knowers, but only after their own interests are looked after.

Socializing Knowers

Socializing knowers are interested in the perspectives of others and very much able to take them into account. Teachers who thrive when working in teams, who can think abstractly about their practice and even sacrifice their own interest to benefit the group are socializing knowers. "These adults are most concerned with understanding other people's feelings and judgments about them and their work" (Drago-Severson, 2008, p. 61). Socializing knowers have substantial capacity for reflection; however, the perspectives of others can be too important. Thus while socializing knowers thrive on teams, they can struggle with having an identity apart from the group. It can be difficult for socializing knowers to challenge their team, department, or group.

Self-Authoring Knowers

Self-authoring knowers have the capacity to think not only about their practice, but also about who they are. Self-authoring knowers "have the developmental capacity to generate their own internal value system, and they take responsibility for and ownership of their own internal authority" (Drago-Severson, 2008, p. 61). Effective school leaders, both informal and formal, are often self-authoring knowers. They can be clear about who they are and what they stand for and, at the same time, expose and explore their fundamental assumptions in a public way. Self-authoring knowers understand that there are tensions associated with the implementation of any professional practice, and they both expect and accept the ambiguity associated with those tensions. Self-authoring knowers understand that there are no easy answers and are suspicious of them when they hear them.

In every school, there are instrumental, socializing, and self-authoring knowers who will experience different learning opportunities in different ways. An instrumental knower might experience an opportunity to complete a collaborative inquiry project with other teachers as a waste of time until she figures out how to get her classroom organized or learns the school's new math program. A socializing knower who thrives on teamwork might be uncomfortable when that work starts to uncover issues of race and class that require her to take a stand independent of her grade-level team or department. The self-authoring knower might find a PowerPoint presentation on bullying too prescriptive and a mechanism to avoid difficult questions. Adult-learning theory suggests that instructional leaders who support adult learning in schools need to understand not only different ways of knowing, but also how the different structures, approaches, and formats that they might use, will be experienced by the different learners who exist in every school.

BEYOND INDIVIDUAL LEARNING

Constructive-developmental theory explains how the ways in which adults make sense out of their experiences can change over time. It gives us a language and conceptual framework that help educators who support adult learning in schools understand a very complex leadership task. Recognizing that adults make meaning in instrumental, socializing, and self-authoring ways helps instructional leaders understand that adults learn in instrumental, socializing, and self-authoring ways (Drago-Severson, 2009). However, in schools it is not just individuals who need to learn. Schools are intricately constructed places, and while a student might have a very productive experience in one classroom, that experience can be undone when the student walks to a classroom across the hall or down the street. Teams, departments, committees, and the wide variety of groups of educators that work in schools also need to learn, and the categories of instrumental, socializing, and self-authoring learning can be applied usefully to the even more complicated and daunting leadership task of supporting group learning.

Schools are places where not only individual educators but also the teams, groups, committees, and departments in which they work, need to learn. A wealth of scholarship and theory argues that effective leadership needs to think not only about individuals but also about the teams in which individuals work and learn (Argyris, 1999; Senge, 2006). Peter Senge's question, "How can a team of committed managers with individual IQs about 120 have a collective IQ of 63?" can be asked of the many teams, departments, and groups in our educational system (Senge, 2006, p. 9). Leading adult learning is not simply a matter of leading individual learning.

Schools are full of hard-working, intelligent, thoughtful, well-educated individuals who are devoted to improving their professional practice for the benefit of their students. Districts typically support educator learning by sending teachers and principals to conferences, offering inservice professional development days, encouraging teachers to pursue graduate study, and a host of other mechanisms. So what's the problem? Senge and many others would argue that it is not just that individuals need to learn, or even that school teams need to learn, but that schools and districts also need to learn (Argyris, 1999; Schein, 2010; Senge, 2006).

Unless a school can learn, the knowledge, insight, and good judgment of each teacher will remain in that teacher's classroom. Even if groups of teachers can learn at high levels, their learning will be confined to their team or department. The school itself needs to learn. Senge describes schools that learn by saying

> It is becoming clear that schools can be re-created, made vital, and sustainably renewed not by fiat or command, and not by regulation, but by taking a *learning orientation*. This means involving everyone in the system in expressing their capabilities together. In a school that learns, people who traditionally may have been suspicious of one another—parents and teachers, educators and local business people, administrators and union members, people inside and outside the school walls, students and adults—recognize their common stake in the future of the school system and the things they can learn from each other. (Senge, McCabe, Lucas, Kleiner, Dutton, & Smith, 2000, p. 5, emphasis in the original)

If organizations—and schools and school districts in particular—do not learn, then they cannot improve.

The need to support the learning not only of individual educators but also of the teams, groups, departments, schools, and districts in which they work complicates the work of instructional leaders. Instructional leaders need to build the learning of every individual in every school, as well as the learning of the teams, departments, and groups found in those schools, and also the school and district themselves. In the supervision process, an elementary principal, for example, needs to think about the learning of individuals in the school. However, that principal also might be concerned that the 2nd-grade team needs to learn more about building classroom communities and the 4th-grade team needs to learn more about working with second language learners. The principal also might think that the whole school needs to learn more about authentic assessment. Learning leaders need to think at many levels about the adult learning it takes to improve teacher practice and increase student learning.

Supporting all this learning is a critical and complicated leadership task; however, it can be useful for learning leaders to apply constructive-developmental theory to make sense of these levels of learning that happen in schools (see Table 1.2). Schools—and the individuals, departments, groups, and teams that are found in them—require different learning at different times. Moreover, considerable literature suggests that a school's capacity for learning is very much connected to its capacity for improvement and for increasing student learning (Bryk et al., 2010; McLaughlin & Talbert, 2006; Stoll & Louis, 2007).

Instrumental Learning in Schools

Some schools—and teams, departments, and districts—demand instrumental learning. They are places and groups where answers, expert knowledge, or technical support are needed. They need to know about managing guided reading groups or teaching in longer blocks of time or implementing an

Table 1.2. Leadership Stance and School Learning Needs

School Learning Needs	Leadership Stance
Instrumental Learning	Leaders understand issues of teaching and learning; they have considerable knowledge about "best practice" and know how to help teachers find necessary expertise.
Socializing Learning	Leaders understand how to build collaborative groups, support reflective practice, and build school cultures that are focused on issues of teaching and learning.
Self-Authoring Learning	Leaders not only understand instructional issues and how to build reflective, collaborative cultures but also take an inquiry stance toward their own practice. Leaders become self-authoring learners themselves.

inquiry-based science program. Leaders who support instrumental learning need to understand learning issues and have expertise about instruction, or they need to be able to easily access that expertise.

The limits of instrumental learning become apparent when educators attempt to put their new learning about formative assessment or differentiated instruction or guided reading or writing across the curriculum into practice. Figuring out what instrumental learning looks like in a real classroom with real students often requires more than knowledge of a concrete process or possession of a specific answer. Instrumental learning helps teachers learn *about* a new practice or strategy but not necessarily *how* to integrate that new practice into their teaching. Instrumental learning does not readily transform practice. Learning a new practice, as opposed to learning *about* the new practice, requires lots of discussion, feedback from colleagues, classroom learning experiments, and collaborative work (McLaughlin & Talbert, 2006; Senge, 2006; Stoll & Louis, 2007). It requires socializing learning.

Socializing Learning in Schools

In schools that require socializing learning, leaders also need expertise, but not only in the content areas. These leaders need expertise in building groups, teams, and schools that are collaborative, reflective, and focused on issues of teaching and learning. Powerful forces—lack of resources, insufficient time, district mandates, and bureaucratic necessities—all conspire against schools becoming collaborative, reflective places. Building such places is an intricate and demanding leadership task. Yet substantial research argues that when schools are reflective, collaborative, learning-focused places, then very good things happen for students (Bryk et al., 2010; Donaldson, 2008; Guskey, 2000; Leithwood et al., 2004; Stoll & Louis, 2007). Socializing learning is worth the trouble.

There are limits to socializing learning as well. Because socializing knowers care very deeply about others, and about the perspective and the wisdom of the group, it can be very difficult for them to challenge the group. Both organizational theory and group theory support the idea that schools, districts, teams, and departments are essentially conservative (Hargreaves & Shirley, 2009; Schein, 2010; Senge, 2006). Simply put, they don't like change and do not always welcome data, conversations, or questions that disturb their equilibrium (Schein, 2010). The result is that socializing learners sometimes can avoid difficult questions about race, class, dropouts, student failure, and equitable educational practice. In schools, the most difficult learning is different from socializing learning. It is a learning that is able to both understand and value the reflective, collaborative strengths of the group and at the same time to maintain a position that challenges the group. This is self-authoring learning.

Self-Authoring Learning in Schools

Supporting self-authoring learning in schools makes even more demands on leadership practice. Self-authoring learners are willing to take the biggest risks, tackle the most difficult questions, and challenge themselves and others the most. To support this learning, a leader needs to not only understand how collaborative, reflective groups are built, but also take the risk to be a self-authoring learner herself—and in a public and transparent way. It seems unlikely that teachers will take the risk to be self-authoring learners, and tackle the most difficult and troubling issues of their practice, unless leaders are also willing to do this. Leaders model self-authoring learning by asking difficult questions, by presenting disconfirming data, and by exposing and exploring their fundamental assumptions in public.

Self-authoring learning is limited by the fact that it can be very risky. Schools and school districts do not always welcome hard questions or disconfirming data. Moreover, because school leaders typically work in organizational cultures that expect school leaders to be problem-solvers who have a good answer to every question, leaders who lead by asking difficult questions and being learners themselves can seem different, unclear, and even weak (Heifetz & Linsky, 2002).

ALONG THE LEARNING CONTINUUM

A useful way to understand the complex demands that supporting adult learning makes on a leader's professional practice is to consider the notion of a "holding environment" (Drago-Severson, 2008; Heifetz & Linsky, 2002).

> A holding environment consists of all those ties that bind people together and enable them to maintain their collective focus on what they are trying to do. All the human sources of cohesion that offset the forces of division and dissolution provide a sort of containing vessel in which work can be done. (Heifetz, Grashow, & Linsky, 2009, p. 155)

In this view, it is the responsibility of leaders—or a teacher or parent, for that matter—to create an environment in which there is enough challenge so that people will take a learning risk, but also enough safety for the learning risk to be manageable.

Leaders create "instrumental" holding environments not only by providing enough expertise, technical support, and content knowledge to reassure learners, but also by challenging adults to work together to take advantage of the knowledge and learning that exists in the schools. Leaders challenge instrumental learners to become socializing learners.

Leaders build "socializing" holding environments both by creating intentional structures that encourage group collaboration and reflection, and also by encouraging the learners to take up difficult questions of practice and take responsibility for the process they use to explore the questions.

Leaders fashion "self-authoring" holding environments for learners by creating structures in which the learners have responsibility both for their learning and for the process. A leader challenges and supports self-authoring learners by becoming one himself, by asking the hard questions, and by resisting the easy answers.

THE ORGANIZATION OF THIS BOOK

Lately, we have been reading books about how students learn, about how they should learn in authentic ways or for deep understanding or by equitable means. We read books about improving student learning by taking into account cognitive science, by planning backwards, by being culturally competent, by teaching in longer blocks of time, by implementing standards-based curricula, and by developing formative assessments. Surely, improving student learning is the right focus. Yet, despite all this emphasis on student learning, in this book we ask how it is possible for students to achieve more and learn in more authentic, equitable ways if teachers, principals, team leaders, superintendents, department chairs—all the adults in schools— also do not learn new ways to teach, to work together, and to think about their profession. How can we reform and even transform schools unless the adults in schools can reform and transform their own practice—unless they can learn?

This book argues that the work of school reform—or improving student learning—is inextricably connected to the learning of the adults who work in schools. No matter how good the new practices, policies, structures, programs, initiatives, curricula, and methods are, they still have to be learned by educators. There is no other way. And it turns out that adults in our schools, like the students, learn in a variety of ways and those ways can change over time. It is not easy.

In the following chapters we explore a simple question that has a complicated answer: How do leaders help teachers learn? This question recognizes that (1) schools get better only when teachers are continually learning about their practice, (2) instructional leadership has a unique responsibility for supporting teacher learning, and (3) instructional leaders need to learn about the work of helping teachers learn. This book attends to the learning that instructional leaders need in order to do their work. It explores the practices, structures, and approaches that leaders can use to support teacher learning as well as the decision making and facilitation needed to make these learning structures effective.

In this chapter, we have described constructive-developmental theory and explained how focusing on adult learning often goes "against the grain" of how schools operate. Chapter 2, "Instrumental Learning in Schools," introduces learning structures and practices that are the least "against the grain" and consequently are often good places to begin to build learning capacity. The learning structures discussed in this chapter can be characterized as particularly supportive of instrumental learners. These structures are a good place to start; they have concrete processes, specific content, and require little experience with reflective practice.

Chapter 3, "Socializing Learning in Schools," examines a series of structures and practices that are more challenging, but also increase the possibility of impacting teacher practice. This chapter on socializing learning in schools describes learning structures that develop reflective, collaborative capacity and require the ability to understand a variety of perspectives. The purpose of these socializing structures is to encourage educators to collaboratively examine their professional practice as a way to improve that practice.

In Chapter 4, "Self-Authoring Learning in Schools," we consider some structures and practices that can be very powerful engines for teacher learning, particularly because they help surface and challenge fundamental notions of teaching and learning. The structures can be characterized as "self-authoring" because they build capacity for reflection on practice, the skills of collaboration, and the ability to take an inquiry stance toward our own fundamental assumptions and beliefs. They are the most powerful learning structures, but they also can be the most challenging to implement. They are rarely a good place to start.

In Chapters 5 and 6, we focus on the learning that leaders need in order to build, deepen, and maximize teacher learning. Chapter 5, "How Leaders Facilitate for Learning," discusses the notion of facilitative leadership and offers some concrete approaches to the work of leading learning. Chapter 6, "How Leaders Design for Learning," takes up a series of questions that leaders need to answer in order to make good design decisions about the structures and practices that they use to promote teacher and school learning.

Chapter 7, the final chapter, "Leading for Learning," argues that the notion of schools as places where adults are necessarily learners leads to a very different, more purposeful, and transformative understanding of a leader's work.

CHAPTER 2

Instrumental Learning in Schools

There are times when schools need to employ instrumental learning. Instrumental learning provides teachers, groups, departments, and schools with concrete, specific ways to build their practice and improve student learning. This chapter provides approaches for addressing individual, small-group, and organizational instrumental learning. What the strategies described in this chapter have in common are clear goals and expectations, transparent processes and procedures, and a focus on specific skills or concrete ideas.

We describe the structures, knowing that instructional leaders will identify the content based on specific teacher or school needs. To demonstrate the strategies and how they serve instrumental learning needs, we provide examples throughout the chapter, and include a focus on two elementary principals (the "Sues"), to show how different schools and school leaders have designed instrumental learning for a variety of learning initiatives and purposes.

In the fall of 2010, Sue Snyder and Sue Charochak, both elementary principals in the Beverly, Massachusetts, public schools, determined that their schools would benefit from learning more about classroom management and building classroom communities. The principals agreed that their schools would be better places for kids if the adults learned about research-based processes and procedures that could be used to build effective and caring classrooms. In this case, the principals decided to teach their schools' teachers about some of the fundamental ideas and techniques used in the Responsive Classroom program (Charney, 1992; Responsive Classroom, 2011).

The principals' strategy was simple. They taught. They worked together to design a series of lessons and learning activities that would help teachers learn more about effective, caring classroom management. They based the design on training they had received in the model, which means they had the requisite knowledge and expertise to design and teach the activities.

In order to teach this important content, "the Sues" (as they are called by other principals in their leadership group) convened their faculty meetings as "classes." A series of faculty meetings was developed using an overarching essential question that headed every faculty meeting agenda: If we expect children to be knowledgeable, responsible, and caring, and to be

> We just figured out that our faculty meetings needed to be classes, and
> we need to be teachers.
>
> —Sue Snyder, Principal,
> Hannah Elementary School, Beverly, Massachusetts

so despite significant obstacles, how will we teach social and emotional skills, attitudes, and values with the same structures and attention that we devote to traditional subjects? They asked the teachers to participate in text-based discussions around emerging research, to form study groups to go deeper into a facet of the model, to engage in jigsaw activities with components of the Responsive Classroom program, and to observe in different classrooms where strategies were being implemented well. Importantly, in every faculty meeting the principals modeled one strategy with the staff, both to demonstrate the strategy and to allow the teachers to experience and then discuss it. At the end of 3 months of working in this way, Sue Charochak said, "In many ways this was one of my greatest successes as a school leader. It's interesting that in order to have my greatest success as a leader, I became a teacher."

In this chapter, we discuss different actions that leaders can take to facilitate instrumental learning for the teachers in their schools. With instrumental learning, the learning taking place is always at the level of the individual teacher. While groups may be experiencing the learning together, for the most part instrumental learning focuses on building teacher learning and practice at the individual level—individual teacher, individual classroom. Any attempt at coherence or a broader school emphasis starts to move into socializing learning, which can be a natural "next place" to go. In the case

Structures That Support Instrumental Learning

- Expert-based professional development
- Instructional coaching
- Using text and multimedia resources
- Study groups
- Walkthroughs
- Mentoring
- Clinical supervision

of the Sues and their planning, they had to decide whether a few teachers needed this learning or was this something that would benefit the whole school. Building instrumental learning in schools recognizes that individual teachers often share common needs for learning, especially based on their shared students and context.

INITIATING INSTRUMENTAL LEARNING

Leaders begin to think about instrumental learning in their school when they ask: What are the instrumental learning needs of our group? Where would individuals or groups benefit from learning specific strategies and methods for teaching and working with students? At any level of an organization—whether a school, district, team, or individual—educators can benefit from learning and using the strategies of instrumental learning.

Organizational instrumental learning may be initiated when a leader or leadership team becomes aware of a needed improvement in practice. In the case of the Sues, they saw a need in their school and took a very instrumental approach to addressing it. Thus the leaders identified a need or opportunity.

Teachers also may initiate instrumental learning. For example, at Lee High School in San Antonio, Texas, teachers asked for more strategies to work with English language learners, especially as they were experiencing an influx of new students from Somalia. Instrumental learning needs and opportunities also can become apparent as groups of teachers with a common focus work together—for example, a grade level, subject area, or team. Instrumental learning becomes a way for teachers to focus on and improve their individual practice. For example, using the same Lee High School example, biology teachers on a level might work together to learn strategies for supporting English language learners as they read and try to make sense of the dense and vocabulary-laden biology textbook.

The Sues decided to focus on classroom management and building effective and caring classrooms. As one of the agendas that the Sues developed for a faculty meeting demonstrates (see Figure 2.1), they used several different strategies in their learning meetings. Furthermore, they were not afraid to position themselves as instructional leaders with expertise and knowledge to share with their teachers. They constructed a series of PowerPoint presentations that were short, informative, and placed at key points in the overall plan for each faculty meeting. Thus, in their plan, instrumental learning came in the form of the leader-developed, expert-based presentations, using texts, instructional coaching via modeled strategies, walkthroughs, and classroom observations of effective practices, as well as a research-based program (the Responsive Classroom program).

Figure 2.1. Instrumental Learning Faculty Meeting Agenda

Agenda

October 6, 2010, 2:15 p.m.

Overarching Essential Question: If we expect children to be knowledgeable, responsible, and caring, and to be so despite significant obstacles, how will we teach social and emotional skills, attitudes, and values with the same structures and attention that we devote to traditional subjects?

Check-In Activity

Essential Question: If we here at Ayers believe, as our mission statement says, that "we will provide a safe, respectful environment for all individuals," how will we respond when students misbehave?

Presentation (PowerPoint): Supporting Positive Behaviors — Part 5

Activity:

Time-Out Video—when students resist time-out

Jigsaw—Discuss video and article in "buddy teacher" groups
- Group 1: read for procedure
- Group 2: read as skeptics
- Group 3: read for benefits
- Group 4: read for preparation necessary, that is, what needs to be done ahead of time?
- Group 5: read considering the role of students in class

Wrap up and closure: "3-2-1" (3 new insights, 2 questions, and 1 new thing I am going to try)

EXPERT-BASED PROFESSIONAL DEVELOPMENT

The Sues had expertise regarding the Responsive Classroom as a result of their training and experience. Therefore, they were able to design and facilitate the learning activities. Expert-based professional development via presenters and consultants is one immediate means by which to initiate instrumental learning in a school (Guskey, 2002; Guskey & Yoon, 2009). Experts can come from within the school context, as with the Sues, or outside of the school. When expert-based professional development occurs, teachers expect to gain "specific, concrete, and practical ideas that directly relate to the day-to-day operation of their classrooms" (Guskey, 2002, p. 382). Therefore, expert-based professional development is an effective way to develop instrumental learning in a school.

Sending teachers to seminars and workshops to gain specific knowledge and expertise is also a way to provide expert-based instrumental learning. The challenge of using remote workshops and seminars is to make sure that teachers will be able to implement the learning in their context. Many teachers want or need implementation support, so leaders will want to think about how to provide that; for example, if they send teachers in groups, the teachers can then work together on implementation, perhaps forming a study group to discuss what is happening in their individual classrooms in terms of successes and challenges. Instructional coaching also can help to support teachers' implementation.

USING MULTIMEDIA RESOURCES FOR INSTRUMENTAL LEARNING

As the Sues' agenda shows, multimedia resources played an important part of their agenda as "texts" to learn from and respond to. Expert-based, instrumental learning often comes in the form of books, articles, web modules, DVDs, or other "texts." Some instructional leaders find it challenging to design learning around the use of a text. The challenge is making the text meaningful and actionable. As Sue said, she had to become a teacher and design the learning experience. Leaders have to figure out not only which texts to use but also how to use them to support instrumental learning. Texts used for instrumental learning purposes need a clear focus on the instrumental learning to be gained. In thinking about how to "teach" the text, instructional leaders can use K–12 instructional strategies such as the Block Party (each person in the group gets a different quote from the text on a strip of paper and then participants are instructed to meet in pairs and talk about their text and do that with several people), Jigsaw (each person in a small group reads a different section of the text and then reports back to the group so that the group can then put the whole piece—the jigsaw puzzle—together), and other text-based protocols and strategies. A resource list of text-based protocols and strategies for using text and other multimedia resources is provided on the School Reform Initiative (2012b) website.

The Sues used texts as part of their overall plan for instrumental learning in a few important ways. They knew that requiring reading in advance would make teachers accountable for their participation. To support the advance reading for learning as well as accountability, they made sure to always give a purpose and focus for the reading. They selected texts that were instrumental, that helped teachers to gain foundational knowledge, and that could serve as a reference tool. The point was not to interpret and discover meaning, as that is socializing learning; rather, the point was to learn "why" and "how to." Having common readings built shared knowledge and language across the school for when teachers were discussing what was taking place in their individual classrooms. Finally, the Sues also used DVD clips as "texts" and the basis for discussion—so the teachers could see something in action and talk about what they saw.

INSTRUCTIONAL COACHING

When the Sues modeled specific practices for teachers at faculty meetings, they were demonstrating the strategies they wanted teachers to learn and implement in their own classrooms. Therefore, they were enacting instructional coaching in the form of modeling. They also provided in-class coaching to support teachers' own use and practice. In that way, they provided instructional coaching in the form of an expert giving feedback about specific practices. Thus, instrumental coaching depends on expert modeling and expert coaching on specific strategies and approaches (Birman, Desimone, Porter, & Garet, 2000; Guskey & Yoon, 2009).

With instructional coaching, teachers have a very practical and pragmatic way to learn. Either they are observing another teacher who has mastered a practice in another classroom or instructional setting, or someone is coming into their classroom to model a particular practice for them to see in action.

This instrumental learning helps teachers to see a practice in action—it is a concrete manifestation of something as opposed to reading or hearing about it, and it takes place in "real time." When it takes place in teachers' own classrooms via a demonstration, it can be especially helpful to teachers because they see it taking place with their own students in their own classrooms and school. This strategy of demonstration teaching by expert teachers is a central component of the Reading and Writing Project led by Lucy Calkins at Teachers College, Columbia University (Teachers College Reading and Writing Project, 2011). The highly regarded program not only provides demonstration teaching but implements it in a sequence of on-site school professional development activities that starts with demonstration teaching, followed by in-class coaching, assessment support, and study groups.

STUDY GROUPS

Study groups involve teachers and leaders coming together to learn about new trends, developments, and practices related to a particular topic (Murphy, 1992; Murphy & Lick, 2004). Study groups offer a structure within which teachers gain new learning by focusing with a group on a specific area of practice about which they will learn. Study groups often meet by grade level or department, although they also may be developed for special interests or needs. In study groups, teachers read, do action research, and share professional knowledge in order to gain and deepen knowledge and expertise. The Sues used study groups as a way for teachers to explore specific aspects of the Responsive Classroom program as well as to discuss how the classroom strategies were working. They designated the study group content, structure, and leadership.

Study groups should be job-embedded, which means they are specific to teachers' school context and work. This is an important instrumental learning feature—study groups are practical, pragmatic, and context-specific. They also are often content-specific, thus the departmental or grade-level organization. When they are more broadly constituted, for example, across the school, they should have a clear focus on a teaching and learning issue. The purpose of teachers' collective participation is to enable them to discuss what they are learning and how it is working in terms of individual classroom implementation (Birman et al., 2000).

What differentiates the study group from a committee or task force is its clear focus on an instructional and/or teacher practice issue. Further, what distinguishes the study group from a professional learning community, which is discussed in the next chapter as a socializing learning activity, is the targeted and limited focus on a specific aspect of practice that teachers implement in their own classrooms.

The study group's structure depends on why the study group is being formed. Leaders might keep the following questions in mind in order to more sharply focus the initiative:

- How will the focus/foci be determined? For example: Will the topics be identified by the teachers or the leaders, or will they emerge from school data? Do teachers select a topic, is there a single topic, or can topics for learning emerge? Who will decide and how?
- How will the groups form and who will lead them?
- How will the study groups be supported by school leaders?
- What will be the role of school leaders? Will they join groups? Have their own? How can they model the learning and participation that might take place?

Finally, while in the case of the Sues everyone was focused on and learning about the Responsive Classroom program, that is not the only way to enact study groups. Study groups might pursue different topics of instrumental learning, tracking their learning and reporting on their progress from time to time. While topics in a school may be the same or may vary, a successful school-based study group initiative provides (1) a standardized process across a school, (2) a well-mapped process with clear expectations so that groups can function without immediate supervision, and (3) a concrete action plan (Easton, 2004). Learning Forward (formerly the National Staff Development Council) and others have developed resources to help instructional leaders design and implement study groups (Learning Forward, 2011; Murphy & Lick, 2006).

WALKTHROUGHS

Walkthroughs are included in this chapter on instrumental learning because they help leaders to assess and build individual teacher and organizational capacity (Cervone & Martinez-Miller, 2007; Protheroe, 2009). Walkthroughs are observations that are short in duration and frequent. They can serve as a means by which to determine what the school needs to learn; they help a leader to take a macro view of a group or school and look beyond any one individual teacher's classroom. As Kathy Bieser, principal of the International School of the Americas in San Antonio, Texas, says, "The best way for me to find out what's going on in classrooms is to get out into classrooms."

It was after doing walkthroughs in their schools that the Sues realized they wanted to target classroom management as a focus for their school's learning. Getting a picture of teacher practice—both successes and challenges—is important when seeking to build instrumental learning in a school.

Walkthroughs are also a way to see whether instrumental learning practices that are the focus of a school initiative are taking hold. For example, as part of their design, the Sues could have continued doing walkthroughs to see how the classroom strategies they were discussing in faculty meetings were taking hold.

Walkthroughs often include some form of feedback. The feedback goes to individual teachers specifically, a group more holistically, or both. For individual feedback, teachers might get a short note or a feedback form letting them know what the observer saw or noted—for example, which specific Responsive Classroom practices were observed in action or in the classroom.

For collective feedback, leaders gather data during their walkthroughs to share with the school faculty in order to provide an idea of where an effort is, or is not, taking hold. That might mean discussing a Responsive Classroom practice in a faculty meeting, doing walkthroughs to see it in practice, and then providing data at the next faculty meeting. Such data might include frequency, effectiveness, challenges, or any other area leaders predetermine. In cases where aggregate data are going to be shared with the faculty, findings should be presented collectively, carefully, and

> In order to support teacher learning in the school, you have to get into classrooms. But you have to have a focus, a reason for being there.
> —Justin Vernon, Principal,
> Roger Clap Innovation School, Boston, Massachusetts

specifically. Being specific does not mean naming individual teachers—it is about describing broadly what's happening in the school and how practices are being implemented.

Walkthroughs are influential in school improvement when they focus on the effects of instruction and serve as a catalyst for schoolwide discussion (Cervone & Martinez-Miller, 2007; Protheroe, 2009). Therefore, the idea would not be to present general data and end things there, but rather to use the data for some kind of further learning. In the context of instructional coaching, walkthroughs do not have to be limited to instructional leaders only. They might include teachers as the observers so that teachers see what is happening more broadly across the school or in specific classrooms where an instructional practice is working well. For example, walkthroughs might relate to a study group or an expert-based professional development initiative.

For example, Kelley Young, Dean of Mathematics at Lee High School, describes how walkthroughs have supported her department's differentiation efforts.

> More and more focus has been placed on differentiation for student success. Many teachers have been told to "do" it, but they don't really have a complete understanding of what that means. The teachers in my department wanted to differentiate more for students and really did not think they were doing it well. I was floored. During my walkthroughs, I had seen them differentiate multiple times as part of their teaching. I was able to point out and celebrate all of the things they were already doing, and give evidence. We were able to change the conversation from what they weren't doing, to what they were, and then focus on how to build on that foundation.

In order for walkthroughs to support instrumental learning, leaders must be certain of the purpose and process. They need to determine (1) a walkthrough focus, (2) a data collection method, and (3) how they are going to make use of the resulting data.

There are many resources for schools and leaders interested in walk-throughs, especially those interested in doing walkthroughs with a team and with a specific focus that is to be reported to a school community. These include Learning Forward (2011) and the Institute for Learning (2011) at the University of Pittsburgh.

There are also other protocols and processes for doing observations in schools similar to walkthroughs. Based on medical school "rounds," City, Elmore, Fiarman, and Teitel (2009) have developed an instructional rounds process for use in schools. Schools invite observers to conduct rounds focused on a specific problem of practice and within the context of a the-ory of action. They describe how to plan, conduct, and debrief the rounds and also provide recommendations so that rounds, like walkthroughs, do not become misused for punitive purposes, confused with supervision, or focused on nonteaching issues. In addition, the School Reform Initiative (2012a) provides protocols for school walks such as the *School Walk*, *Ghost Walk*, and *Collaborative Ghost Walk*. Finally, a reminder of what walk-throughs and these other observational strategies should *not* be: a tool for appraisal, a check for compliance, or a "gotcha" for teachers.

As Kelley Young, Dean of Mathematics at Lee High School, notes,

> One of the best things about walkthroughs is the ability to see all of the good things that teachers and students are doing in the classroom and then share with others in the department. Teachers often do not appreciate all they bring individually to the classroom and how different all of us are. They have a tendency to think everyone is doing what they are doing so it doesn't occur to them what they could share that would help others. Seeing all of the different teachers and their practices and being able to share those with others in the department has been invaluable.

MENTORING

Given the "greening" of the teaching profession with the retirement of Baby Boomers and teacher turnover, instructional leaders need to support the instrumental learning of new and novice teachers (Ingersoll & Merrill, 2010). This includes both teachers new to the profession as well as teach-ers new to a school or context. New teachers need instrumental learning in order to continue developing their practice. Participating in schoolwide instrumental learning also serves to include and integrate them in the school culture and professional community. Focusing on new teachers is, as Ellen Moir and her colleagues at the New Teacher Center describe, "an important leverage point for increasing teacher, and teaching, quality throughout the system" (Moir, Barlin, Gless, & Miles, 2009, p. 1).

Among any group of new teachers there will be instrumental, social-izing, and self-authoring learners, as discussed in Chapter 1. Instrumental learners have concrete needs and want specific processes, socializing learners focus on others and group needs, and self-authoring learners are reflective about themselves and their context. Research on effective new teacher induction tells us that novice teachers benefit from a range of pro-fessional learning experiences, not just instrumental learning (Moir et al., 2009). Yet as a group, new teachers will have immediate, practical, and concrete instrumental learning needs that instructional leaders can antici-pate. This includes making sure new teachers know how to enact proce-dures—for example, taking attendance using the online system, turning in the lunch count, figuring out the web-based grading program, setting up parent conferences, and the usual litany of other teacher procedures. It also means taking into account teaching and learning needs related to a school's curricular programs, pedagogical expectations, and classroom management expectations.

Many schools tend to use multiple approaches to build instrumental learning, such as new teacher meetings for collective learning and mentors for individual support (Easton, 2004). Both meetings and mentors can pro-vide socializing learning as well as instrumental learning. Collective new teacher meetings might focus on sharing information, particularly "how to" or "by when" information regarding tasks and responsibilities. For exam-ple, providing technological instruction and support for learning adminis-trative tasks is an important instrumental learning need.

Individualized support for instrumental learning often comes in two forms: (1) supervision by an administrator (which we address in the next section on clinical supervision) and (2) the support of a mentor teacher assigned to the new teacher. Mentor teachers are experienced teachers who provide instrumental learning in terms of procedures, instructional strat-egies, and "how to" knowledge as well as affective support. Often this teacher is physically or organizationally "nearby"—a teacher in a neighbor-ing classroom, someone on the same grade level, or someone in the same department. Robbins (1999) explains that the benefits of mentoring extend beyond practical help or welcoming support: "After the nuts and bolts of life within the organization are shared, the focus on mentoring may cen-ter on curriculum, standards, instructional practices, classroom climate, or classroom management issues. The desired consequence of this support: improved student learning" (p. 40).

Leaders not yet doing so might consider mentor training to help men-tors enact this unique role. Another readily available step would be to bring the mentors together with the facilitator of the new teacher meetings to talk about what they are doing and how things are going from an instrumental learning perspective—what do the new teachers need to learn and how can that learning be provided? This helps the collective meetings and individualized support to work together and "inform" one another (Easton, 2004).

While specific instrumental learning structures for new teachers are important, and new teachers should participate in schoolwide instrumental learning activities with their colleagues, we also know that participating in the socializing and self-authoring structures, such as learning communities, teacher-led inquiry, lesson study, and critical friends groups, which will be described in Chapters 3 and 4, is important as well. These experiences promote socializing and self-authoring learning in groups that usually consist of both novice and more experienced teachers. Furthermore, Chapter 6 addresses specific intergenerational dynamics that leaders should anticipate when designing approaches for school learning. The chapter includes a focus on knowing teachers well, including new and novice teachers who are considered part of "Generation Y," and it provides specific approaches for working with Gen Y teachers as well as ways to think about the cultural dynamics that might emerge between these novice and more veteran teachers.

CLINICAL SUPERVISION

We want to make a connection in this chapter to something that is likely already happening in schools—teacher supervision. For those leaders with supervisory roles and responsibilities, supervision is a tool that can support teachers' learning. Not all instructional leaders have supervisory roles and responsibilities; when those who do have such roles envision their responsibility as both evaluative and developmentally oriented, as opposed to simply evaluative, they can support teachers in their instrumental learning and practice.

Clinical supervision is a form of supervision that might help leaders make some instrumental learning assessments as well as target some instrumental learning support. Clinical supervision occurs when leaders help teachers identify areas in which they can improve their practice (Glickman, Gordon, & Ross-Gordon, 2010; Pajak, 2003; Sergiovanni & Starratt, 2002). As Sergiovanni and Starratt (2002) describe, "Clinical supervision can take many forms but invariably involves an in-depth examination and careful study of selected teaching issues, the collection of data that helps the teacher understand these issues, and the development of improved practice" (p. 226). The leader's role is to help identify the teaching issues, collect and present data so that they will help the teacher to look at her practice and student learning, and make recommendations.

Clinical supervision consists of the following steps (Sergiovanni & Starratt, 2002):

1. leader (supervisor) has a pre-conference with the teacher to prepare for the classroom observation and determine a focus for it
2. classroom observation
3. leader (supervisor) analyzes the observation notes and prepares recommendations, advice, materials, and strategies to share in the conference
4. post-observation conference between the leader and teacher
5. leader (supervisor) reflects on the conference

Establishing these specific procedures is critical when building instrumental learning. Ambiguity regarding the process gets in the way of teachers' learning and participation. The pre-conference is important because it builds shared understanding and agreement regarding the purpose and focus of the observation. The post-conference helps to identify specific next steps in terms of learning and practice. Next steps might include expert-based professional development, instructional coaching via demonstration teaching, observations of other teachers, or any other instrumental learning strategies. Providing leadership for teachers' instrumental learning requires instructional leadership from those doing the clinical supervision—finding answers and resources—whether that means providing the specific expertise themselves or finding expert resources for the teacher.

Building on this idea of instructional leadership, we offer clinical supervision as a specific strategy for instructional leaders in both evaluative and nonevaluative positions. Many instructional leaders in schools have been selected for their role as a department chair, dean, peer coach, mentor, level leader, or other teacher leadership role based on their strong curricular or pedagogical expertise; yet these leaders might have little preparation for what it means to and how to coach and support teachers (who are often colleagues and peers in the school) in their development (Zepeda & Kruskamp, 2007). These leaders are in a unique role—neither supervisor nor peer—often with little guidance regarding possible practices. Further, there is often some confusion regarding the role—are there evaluative aspects of the work and role, has evaluation truly been separated from facilitating teacher development (Glickman, 2002)? Any instructional leader, whether a formal evaluator or not, will find that clinical supervision can support teachers' individualized instrumental learning, especially when it: (1) follows a clear and well-communicated process, (2) focuses on instrumental learning goals and activities, and (3) provides expertise and resources for that learning.

SUPPORTING INSTRUMENTAL LEARNING:
IMPLICATIONS FOR LEADERSHIP

Pursuing instrumental learning as a school is important, not only for the learning teachers gain but also because it might begin to build capacity for more collaborative learning in an instrumental-socializing way (Drago-Severson, 2009). Moving from instrumental to socializing learning can be the next progression for a school's learning. It also can be a "fall-back" for schools experiencing extreme stress, as instrumental learning can be a "safer" way to learn as long as it is not a place to get stuck (Drago-Severson, 2009; Knefelkamp & David-Lang, 2000). So, whether as a way to move toward socializing learning, or to gain new knowledge for practice, instrumental learning has a place in individual and organizational learning—there are simply times when individuals and/or the school need to develop new or different capacity for specific, concrete, curricular, pedagogical, and school practices.

The Role of the Leader

Across all of these strategies and possibilities, it is important to remember that instrumental learning requires providing teachers with expertise, concrete answers, and specific processes that they can enact in their individual practice and in their classrooms. Leaders must provide "an answer" or find a place where the learner will get one. They need to see themselves as teachers—able to design and provide learning experiences that will develop teachers' knowledge and skill.

Therefore, the key role for leaders is to find the expertise that will help their teachers and their school. Pankake and Moller (2007) describe this role of the leader as that of a "matchmaker" who helps teachers to identify learning needs and then "matches" those needs to learning opportunities. Principals have to "match-make" on an individual level and on a school-wide level as well. This includes finding quality programs, research-based strategies, effective consultants, and informative texts, as well as using or adapting the described structures and processes.

Challenges for Leaders

The good news is that instrumental learning can have direct benefit for teachers and, importantly, for student learning (Guskey & Yoon, 2009). The limit is that it usually involves individual teachers working on their own practice in their own classroom or setting. This is true whether a leader is providing whole-school instrumental learning or trying to support individual teacher learning. The focus and effort are usually on the individual teacher's classroom and practice. The Sues knew that if all of the teachers in their schools were working to improve the climate and learning environment of classrooms, the school would benefit; however, the learning of the school was primarily limited to individual teacher practice. It is hard to work for coherence and meaning when teachers are working to master specific knowledge and strategies in their individual classrooms. "What" and "how to" can take a school only so far.

The significant challenge in creating instrumental learning is its design. As the Sues said, they had to plan for teacher learning and then enact that plan. Leading for instrumental learning means taking on a design role focused on instrumental content and processes. Leaders who are instrumental learners themselves likely will enjoy taking on this role of providing informational learning and resources for teachers. Socializing and self-authoring leaders will need to resist the temptation to provide socializing or self-authoring learning experiences when trying to build individual or school learning that is instrumental. Related to that, leaders have to anticipate the pushback of socializing or self-authoring learners for whom instrumental learning will be challenging.

CHAPTER 3

Socializing Learning in Schools

*In order to learn more and improve our practice, we have to
dig deeper into what we do, what our kids need, and what we
already know. We need to learn from each other.*

*—Doug Lyons, Principal,
Parker Middle School, Reading, Massachusetts*

Often the answers to the questions that teachers are wondering about
or struggling with can be found right down the hall. In many schools
there are teachers who are exceptional teachers of writing, skilled at
classroom management, wonderful at engaging students, adept at integrating technology, or expert in coaching students to think mathematically. There is a lot of knowledge, wisdom, expertise, and good practice
in every school. To become better places for students, some schools
are ready to explore the practice-related knowledge that already exists
within their hallways. In other words, schools need to employ socializing learning so that educators can learn from one another in ways that
make them better practitioners.

In this chapter we share an array of practices and processes that support
reflection, collaboration, and exploration of multiple points of view, which
are foundational to socializing learning. These strategies ask educators to
"settle in," develop long-term relationships, and explore the challenging
craft of teaching and learning (McDonald, Mohr, Dichter, & McDonald,
2007; McLaughlin & Talbert, 2006).

PLANNING FOR SOCIALIZING LEARNING

When Doug Lyons became the principal of Parker Middle School in Reading,
Massachusetts, he began asking a few simple questions: What do we want
to learn about in order to do a better job for our kids? What do we already
know? Who knows it? He discovered in the responses to his questions that
teachers *were* interested in pursuing a wide range of questions connected to
their practice: How can we engage kids better? How can we help kids who
struggle to learn in a typical classroom? How can we do a better job with

assessment? How do we better use technology to support student learning? These were some of the questions that teachers struggled with and wanted to learn more about.

When the teachers in the school started looking at what they needed to learn, it became apparent that they already knew a lot but did not have ways to share their knowledge and their questions related to improving their practices. Doug and the other members of the school's Instructional Leadership Team, including the assistant principal and the grade-level team leaders, took on the task of creating ways for teachers to learn from the wisdom and good practice already in the building. In other words, how could they support socializing learning?

GOING AGAINST THE GRAIN

As it turned out, supporting socializing learning was more complicated than it sounded. Although teachers in most schools have considerable expertise and wisdom, the culture of schools tends to keep teachers in their classrooms and their practice private. Schools are not typically collaborative, reflective places that are able to persistently focus on issues of teaching and learning (Hargreaves & Shirley, 2009; Lieberman & Miller, 2008; Schmoker, 2006). The educators at Parker Middle School worked to change this convention.

The Instructional Leadership Team began to use faculty meetings to talk together about teaching and learning. They created structures for collaboration where teachers who had experience with a topic or practice shared with those who wanted to learn. Eventually every professional development day was devoted to a schoolwide inquiry into themes such as integrating technology into teaching practice. They also used protocols to guide these learning-focused conversations, and they became skilled at facilitating them. As the school became more comfortable taking a collaborative learning approach, the faculty took on more challenging topics and incorporated more demanding processes that required them to give one another feedback and build consensus about good teaching. In other words, they shifted the focus from isolated, individual practice toward a collective emphasis on improving teaching and learning.

Doug was clear about his role in the process. He was not the content expert. His role was to put in place structures to support teachers learning with one another, encouraging teachers to share what they knew and make transparent what they needed to learn, directing resources to support collaborative work, and creating a school that had the capacity for socializing learning. Doug summarized the learning process in this way: "At the end of the day it is about learning—student learning and adult learning. Students need to learn, teachers need to learn, and I need to learn. But it does not happen by accident. Collaborative work does not occur without careful planning and scaffolding."

SUPPORTING SOCIALIZING LEARNING: STRATEGIES AND PROTOCOLS

Doug knew that socializing learning would require providing teachers access to the expertise and practice that existed within the school. Parker Middle School used many of the following strategies and protocols to carve out time and opportunity for teachers to share practice, give and receive feedback, participate equally, and reflect on their practice and learning: (1) learning with texts, (2) looking at student work, (3) looking at adult work, (4) observing colleagues, (5) creating learning communities, and (6) engaging in collaborative supervision.

LEARNING WITH TEXTS

Structuring conversations around a piece of text (printed in a publication or heard in a video) is a strategy to consider early in the movement toward socializing learning. Learning with a text is a familiar way to access expert knowledge from outside resources. In Chapter 2 we described how "the Sues," colleagues and principals at two elementary schools in Beverly, Massachusetts, used texts as part of their instructional plan. In that instance their goal was to use texts to learn "how to" do something or gain specific knowledge. The goal of this socializing version of learning with texts is not to figure out a particular answer but rather to come to see the variety of understandings, perspectives, and assumptions in a group.

At Parker Middle School, Doug often incorporated text-based discussions in faculty meetings with the intent to not only build knowledge but also lay the groundwork for socializing learning. He chose texts as a beginning place because he wanted to use a familiar resource when he was introducing a new way of learning. Doug found that using particular types of protocols helped to ensure that the text discussion resulted in socializing learning. We will discuss two text-based protocols that Doug introduced and used regularly, the *Final Word* and the *Four "A"s Text Protocol*.

The *Final Word* Protocol

The *Final Word* (n.d.) protocol can be used to explore various kinds of text and can be particularly effective when introducing a potentially challenging idea (McDonald et al., 2007). The protocol is designed to give individual people an opportunity to present their ideas, understandings, and perspective, and then to have their points of view enhanced or expanded by listening to the responses of their colleagues (see Figure 3.1 for a description of the protocol). The goal is to gain a deeper understanding of the text.

Figure 3.1. The Final Word Protocol

Getting Started:

The *Final Word* process moves in rounds around the group.

Each round requires about 8 minutes (in a group of 3–5).

The group sits in a circle. After reading the text, each person silently identifies one or two of the most significant quotes from the text and underlines or highlights them.

Rounds:

As the round begins, a person in the group reads the quote that "struck her most" from the text, referring to where the quote is in the text so that everyone can read it. Then for 3 minutes she describes why that quote stood out for her. Why does she agree/disagree with the quote? What questions does she have about the quote? What issues does it raise?

Continuing around the circle each person has 1 minute to respond to the person's quote and what she said about it. The purposes of the responses are to expand on the presenter's thinking about the quote, provide a different look at the quote, and/or wonder about the presenter's assumptions about the quote and the issues it raises.

After everyone in the circle has responded, the person who began has the "final word." In 1 minute she responds to what has been said. Now what is she thinking? What is her reaction to what she has heard?

A new round begins. The next person in the circle shares his quote and has 3 minutes to speak, followed by 1-minute responses from the other group members. The rounds continue until everyone in the group has had an opportunity to share and respond.

Debriefing & Reflection:

The process closes with a reflection on the ideas, insights, or questions that arose from the discussion and a debriefing of the process.

Note: It is important that the facilitator (or a designated timekeeper) attends to the time in each step of the process and ensures that the groups move through the rounds.

The *Four "A"s Text Protocol*

The *Four "A"s* (n.d.) *Text Protocol* explores a text in light of one's own values and perceptions. Again, the purpose is to expand a group's understanding of a text, not to come to an agreement (see Figure 3.2 for a description of the protocol).

Figure 3.2. The *Four "A"s Text* Protocol

Getting Started:

The *Four "A"s* process moves in rounds around
the group. The group sits in a circle.

Each round of questions takes about 5 minutes or about
a minute per participant (in a group of 5), plus an
additional 10 minutes for the final two steps.

After reading the text silently, the group highlights the text,
writing notes in the margins or on Post-it® notes in response
to the following four questions. (You can add to or adapt
the A's.) Each question is allotted at least one round.
- What Assumptions does the author of the text hold?
- What do you Agree with in the text?
- What do you want to Argue with in the text? (or,
  What do you want to Ask the author)?
- What parts of the text do you want to Aspire to (or, Act upon)?

Rounds:

In the first round, each person identifies one assumption
in the text, citing the page number.

The process continues in rounds with each person citing each of
the remaining A's, taking them one at a time—What do you
want to agree with, argue with, and aspire to in the text?

After exploring all of the questions, the group has an open discussion,
often framed around a question posed by the facilitator. The
group's discussion explores the implications of the text for their
work—"What does this mean for our work with our students?"

Debriefing & Reflection:

The session ends with a debriefing on the process.

Both the Final Word and the Four "A"s protocols offer a forum for teachers to share their points of view, understandings, and values with colleagues. The protocols' structure requires educators to engage in the skills and habits of socializing learning. These types of expansive discussions can build shared language, understandings, values and beliefs, and standards of practice—all essential to building a community of socializing learning (McLaughlin & Talbert, 2006).

Each of these processes requires careful selection of a text that offers substantive content. In addition, they call for thoughtful and diligent facilitation to lead the group, within a specified time frame, through the series of steps in the particular order described above. Care and attention are necessary to ensure that the discussions do not detour into a debate to determine the rightness of a particular point of view, attempt to reach consensus, or revert to an "open discussion" that is really a conversation between a few members. One of the challenges for socializing learners is to express points of view that might differ from those of valued colleagues and to live with the ambiguity and tensions that might arise when uncovering these differences. Well-facilitated protocols can help socializing learners navigate these demands.

A crucial phase or step in these protocols, as in all of the ones described throughout this book, is the debriefing, of both the content and the process, that takes place at the end. As mentioned earlier, Doug frequently facilitated these text protocols from the front of the room during a schoolwide faculty meeting. As a way to explicitly support the multiple layers of learning embedded in this socializing learning experience, he led the whole-group debrief of the content—What did we learn from the text and from sharing and hearing multiple perspectives?—and also the process—What did we learn about how the protocol supported and challenged our discussions and us? What do we want to remember to incorporate the next time we use this process? This kind of debriefing process offers a platform from which to identify and develop the insights and dispositions of socializing learning.

LOOKING AT STUDENT WORK

Just as there are several protocols for looking at and learning from text together in ways that support socializing learning, there are also processes for looking at and learning from student work. The *Collaborative Assessment Conference (CAC)* protocol (Seidel, 1998) focuses on looking at and learning from the work of a student (or a group of students), so the student work becomes the "text." The CAC is unlike most of the "looking at student work" that typically is done in schools, such as an individual teacher in his classroom grading papers (see Appendix A for the full protocol). It asks a

> The sole purpose of our conversations with colleagues is about practice. Prior to our use of protocols, we were always having the same conversations and they didn't impact my teaching. I had no idea of the benefit I could get by de-privatizing my practice.
> —Cathy O'Connell, Assistant Principal,
> Parker Middle School, Reading, Massachusetts

group of educators not to assess the quality or accuracy of the work, but rather to carefully delve into what it might reveal about the learning of the student who produced it.

The *Collaborative Assessment Conference* Protocol

The *CAC* is a way for educators to come to know and understand students through the work they produce. It offers an opportunity for a teacher to see a student (occasionally, a group of students) through the eyes of colleagues and to consider other perspectives or interpretations of a student's work. The protocol is grounded in careful description of student work. Student work samples that are open-ended and provide some choice in their responses are often rich artifacts for a *CAC*. Writing samples, three-dimensional models or other visual representations, end-of-unit projects, exhibitions, or formative assessment activities are among the student work that might be presented in a *CAC*.

The *CAC* proceeds through a series of steps that lead to a discussion about a student: What are the strengths and struggles of this student? What is the student working on or trying to accomplish in this work? What are the implications of this student's work for teaching and learning practices? Often the protocol ends with a discussion of the beliefs or assumptions about teaching and learning that surfaced during the process. Uncovering these assumptions can elicit discussion and reflection about broader issues related to teaching and learning among the group's members.

The protocol begins with the presenting teacher sharing copies of a student work sample with the group members. The presenting teacher provides neither context nor background for the work of the student who produced it. The facilitator of the process then poses a series of questions or "rounds" to lead the group through a careful examination of the work. The presenter silently takes notes during this time and does not participate in the rounds.

Beginning with description, the group is asked to literally describe what is seen. For example, in a group looking at student writing, a participant might start the descriptive round by saying: "In the first paragraph, the student writes, 'Thousands of students are being bullied in our schools every day.'" Another participant might say, "Throughout the paper, I see the words 'bully', 'bullies', and 'bullying' spelled conventionally. I see the word bullied spelled 'bullyed' in a nonconventional way." If an evaluation or judgment emerges—"this is a well-organized essay"—the facilitator asks the person to offer evidence to support the assessment. That person might provide supporting description such as: "The first paragraph includes a thesis statement and the last summarizes the ideas."

Following the description phase, the group is asked to raise questions about the work or the student(s). Group members contribute any questions they might have about the student, the assignment, circumstances in which the work was created, and so on. In this round, participants might ask, "I wonder if this is a final draft?" and "Is this document the student's first effort at a problem-solution essay?" and "How was the topic chosen?"

The group then moves to speculate about what the student is working on or trying to accomplish, for example, "The student seems to be working on using data to describe the problem in a problem-solution essay," "The student seems to be incorporating varying sentence structures," and "The student appears to be working on filling more than one page when writing an essay."

Following the speculation step, the presenting teacher enters back into the discussion after listening and taking notes, sharing with the group his perspective on the student's work. The teacher describes the work as he sees it, responds to one or more of the questions that were raised, and comments on anything unexpected that he heard in the previous rounds: "I had not noticed the number and variety of sentence structures that the student incorporated. It was interesting to hear you note that the student incorporated elements of a problem-solution essay because we have not worked on that particular structure in a while. I'm wondering now if this student thinks that essays have to be more than one page long and so has repeated himself in paragraphs 3 and 4 just to add length. We've really been working on covering a topic thoroughly, but I'm thinking that this student—and maybe some others—has interpreted that to mean that more is always better."

The entire group then turns to a discussion about the implications about teaching and learning that this process has raised. This discussion might include ways to support the particular student whose work was presented. As the discussion turns to the beliefs or assumptions about students, teaching, and learning that the process helped to surface, the participants have an opportunity to draw implications for their collective practice from the specific experience of looking at student work.

The *Collaborative Assessment Conference* ends with a whole-group debrief and reflection on the teachers' experiences related to issues raised in the *CAC* and their reaction to the process itself.

Using protocols to publicly examine teacher and student work supports participants in thoughtfully putting in place changes in their individual teaching practices. But it is the shift in focus from improving individual practice to improving collective practice that engages the participants of these protocols in socializing learning. Through the insights and discussion that emerge as a result of these protocols, colleagues uncover where their practices and understandings align and where they don't. They can then begin to build shared understanding and put in place changes in their collective practice. Participating in looking at student work over time, and collectively using the learning gained, can create instructional and curricular coherence across grade levels, content areas, and even schoolwide.

LOOKING AT ADULT WORK

Collaboratively looking at adult work is frequently focused on either improving a piece of professional work using the *Tuning* protocol (Allen, 1998; McDonald, 1993) or examining a dilemma of practice using the *Consultancy* protocol (Thompson-Grove, Evans, & Dunne, n.d.).

The *Tuning* Protocol

The *Tuning* protocol is a structured process that allows a teacher to gather the multiple perspectives of colleagues on a piece of work for the purpose of improving it, refining it, or bringing it more "in tune" with her stated goals or purposes (see Appendix B for the full protocol). The protocol follows a series of steps that include presentation of work, gathering additional information, forming and sharing feedback, reflection by the presenting teacher, and debrief and reflection by the group. The following description illustrates how a *Tuning* protocol might take place.

When using the *Tuning* protocol, the presenting teacher brings an assignment, assessment, lesson plan, or other teaching artifact, along with her goals and purposes, to a group of colleagues for feedback.

The presenting teacher initially describes the context in which the work was created and offers a focusing question to guide the feedback of the group. For example, at Serna Elementary School in San Antonio, which is focused on mathematics instruction, a teacher might bring a lesson plan and ask her colleagues: "What evidence do you see that this lesson plan addresses the areas of need identified by our mathematics assessment?" The participants listen quietly and take notes during the presentation.

Following the teacher's presentation, participants ask clarifying questions of the presenter to gain additional information or insight about the context or circumstances in which the work was developed or about the students involved.

Next, the participants quietly examine the work, noting where they think the work is in alignment or "in tune" with the goal that the presenting teacher offered and where there may be gaps between the work and the stated goal or purpose. With the presenting teacher listening in, taking notes, and not responding, the participants offer first warm and then cool feedback.

Warm feedback includes affirmation that highlights the ways in which the work is in alignment or in tune. Warm feedback offers the presenting teacher not only corroboration but also insight as to the strengths in the work that could be built upon: "I see that students are given choices of manipulatives and other tools they can use to practice a skill several times during the lesson." Cool feedback often is given in the form of a question or a wondering about what might be missing from the piece of work or how it might be improved to bring it into tune with the stated goal or purpose: "I wonder how the lesson accommodates students with different reading abilities."

After the feedback, the presenting teacher enters the conversation and has the opportunity to share her reflections on what she has heard and how the feedback might shape her practice and perceptions. The participants are silent during this reflection.

The *Tuning* ends with a whole-group debrief and reflection on both the content of the conversation—What are we thinking about our own practices as a result of taking part in this protocol? What does this experience suggest about our grade-level assessment processes? What more do we need to know?—as well as the process—How did this protocol support our conversation and learning? What went well? What do we want to remember for next time?

The *Tuning* protocol affirms the strengths and good practices of the presenting colleague. It assures her that she is on the right track. And, it provides constructive ways to revise or refine her work. The debriefing at the close offers the whole group two particular opportunities for learning. First, by debriefing the process, the group develops the skills and practice of collaborative learning. Second, the group's reflection on the implications of the conversation for their own practices can bring to light issues of teaching and learning for individuals, grade levels or content areas, and the school as a whole.

The *Consultancy* Protocol

When using a *Consultancy* protocol, an individual or a group brings to colleagues a particular professional dilemma or issue that the individual or group members can't figure out. Because teaching is complex work, teachers have complex dilemmas regarding student learning and their professional work that they need to tackle with their colleagues. The aim of the group's discussion is not to "solve" the problem for the presenter. Rather, in a *Consultancy*, the goal is to help the presenter think differently about her dilemma, perhaps by better understanding its complexity, so that she might gain new insights or see new possibilities for action. It is this goal of the "consultancy," or consultative experience, to expand understanding and gain insight through hearing other perspectives that aids the presenting teacher in resolving her problem and results in engaging all of the participants in socializing learning.

The *Consultancy* also follows a series of steps, some of which are similar to those in the *Tuning* and others that are unique. Steps include presentation of work, gathering additional information, posing probing questions, discussion, reflection by presenting teacher, and debrief and reflection by the group (see Appendix C for the full *Consultancy* protocol). The following description illustrates a *Consultancy* as it might occur.

During the first step of the *Consultancy*, the presenter gives an overview of the dilemma with which she is struggling and frames a question to focus the group's discussion. The group is silent during the presentation, perhaps taking notes.

Following the presentation, a short time is devoted to asking the presenter clarifying questions. These are questions that will help the group better understand the circumstances and context surrounding the dilemma, for example, "How were the students grouped?," "How much time did the project take?," and "What resources did the students have available?"

Probing questions follow the clarifying questions. These are unique in that their purpose is to help the presenter discern her thinking about the problem. Probing questions help analyze the dilemma and help the presenter think differently about it. "Why do you think this is the case? What if the opposite were true? Then what?" and "What do you think the students who are involved might say about this issue?" The presenting teacher considers each question and may respond to some or all of them, but there is no discussion during this step of the process.

The group then talks with one another about the dilemma while the presenter silently listens and takes notes. The facilitator may offer a series of questions to frame the discussion: "What did we hear? What didn't we hear that might be relevant? What assumptions might be operating? What questions does the dilemma raise for us? What might we do if faced with a similar dilemma?"

Following the discussion, the presenter reflects on what she has heard that particularly resonated with her. This is an opportunity for her to share what she is now thinking after participating in the process and hearing her colleagues tackle her dilemma.

The *Consultancy* ends with the whole group reflecting on the insights and understandings they gained. How did the process work? Was there anything particularly challenging about this process? What helped us to stay focused on the dilemma? What insights about our own individual or collective practice did we gain? Are there implications for our school that emerged?

OBSERVING COLLEAGUES

Another form of looking at and learning from teacher work and practice occurs when teachers observe one another teaching. Engaging in peer observation recognizes that teachers can learn with and from one another. Improving practice by publicly sharing practice stands in strong contrast to the long-standing assumption of teaching as a solitary endeavor (Little, 1990; Lortie, 1975).

When thinking about peer observation, school leaders need to clearly communicate that the purpose is to learn from one another and *not* to evaluate one another. And like all the other collaborative practices of socializing learning, peer observation requires leaders to put in place trustworthy strategies to support and promote equality, reciprocity, reflection, and dialogue—key components in successful learning among educators (Knight, 2011).

The *First Classroom Visits* Process

First Classroom Visits (n.d.) offers an entry point to peer observation. A school leader facilitates and coordinates the entire process, from set-up to reflection and debriefing. There are some key understandings that can help leaders to set up and support this process:

- There is no expectation that a teacher will change her lesson to meet the needs of the observing teacher— the assumption is that the observation of a class will yield new learning/perspective for the observer.
- The observer is there to learn, not to evaluate or give feedback to the observed teacher.
- The observing teacher will share what is learned with the teacher being observed.
- The reflection and debrief support individual and group learning.

Prior to the visits, each observing teacher poses a question related to his own teaching and learning to guide the visit. For example, How can I better facilitate classroom discussions so that students are building on one another's ideas instead of looking to me? Or, My explanations of compound fractions seem to confuse rather than clarify. What might I do differently? The teachers, with the help of a school leader, identify colleagues to observe who can help them think about their questions of practice. It is expected that the observing teachers will make notes during the observation and use these notes to reflect on their resulting learning. Once all the visits have taken place, the leader facilitates a collective discussion among the participants about the learning that emerged from the visits; the process of the observations; what the individual learning might suggest for the practices of the group, grade level, or even the school; and how this learning might guide and inform future peer observations.

When Parker Middle School first set up peer observation visits, Doug, the principal, and Cathy O'Connell, the assistant principal, developed a bank of release class periods during which teachers could visit classrooms to observe colleagues. They also set the school goal of "developing audiences for students' work beyond the classroom" as the focus for the first visits. They found that when they provided time and structure, more teachers were willing to participate. These classroom visits offered the Parker faculty a low-risk opportunity to deprivatize their teaching practice while affirming their efforts to meet a schoolwide goal. The peer observations brought to light the variety of good practices in the school and among the teachers. These initial observations shifted the reliance on outside expert knowledge by highlighting the know-how that existed within the school. The reflections and debriefing following the observations provided a forum for talking about how to make practices more coherent and aligned across the school.

The *Focus Point* Protocol

The *Focus Point* protocol (n.d.) offers another type of peer observation structure. In this approach, a teacher identifies a question about her practice and then asks a colleague to observe her teaching to help her collect data about what is seen and offer feedback on that particular aspect of her practice. *Focus Point* differs from the *First Classroom Visits* process in that colleagues are observing to give one another feedback, and therefore the observations are inherently more risky for the observer and the observed. To be successful, participating teachers need to have some experience, skill, and comfort in observing as well as giving and receiving feedback. Engaging in other opportunities to observe in one another's classrooms, perhaps using the *First Classroom Visits* process, may be a way to prepare for focused observations. Participation in protocol sessions such as the *Tuning* or the *Collaborative Assessment Conference*, as either a presenter or responder, also can provide experience and skill in observation, giving and receiving feedback, and reflection—key components in these observations. Of course, like all of these strategies, focused observations require that the leader support the participating teachers in setting norms that support the observations as well as providing assistance with logistics, including time for a meeting prior to the observation, the observation itself, and the debriefing meeting following.

Similar to the focus of a *Tuning*, the teacher being observed asks the observer to focus on a particular aspect of her practice. During a meeting between the observing and observed teachers prior to the observation, the teacher who will be observed provides context for the observation as well as a focusing question that will guide it. For example, a teacher might share information about the students, the curriculum, and the particular lesson that will be observed, and then give the focus for the observation. The teacher might ask, "Would you note how I engage students during the class period? I am wondering if I am engaging all my students equally."

Following the pre-conference, the observer comes into the classroom at the agreed-upon time and observes, focusing on the teacher's question or point of interest—and only that focus. The observing teacher makes notes during the observation that might include descriptions of instances related to the focusing question—noting where the teacher stands during the class period, who speaks and who doesn't, who has his or her hand raised, who is called on, and so on. The observer also might jot down questions that he might want to raise during the debriefing or reflection phase of the process: "Are the girls who sit in the front row always quiet? Do the students usually finish the assignments before the end of the class period?" Initially observations might last about 15–20 minutes; they could become longer as both the observed and the observing teachers become more comfortable.

Following the observation, the two colleagues meet to discuss the observation, again for a short amount of time, about 10 minutes or so when starting out. The teacher who was observed usually begins by giving her impression of the class session that was observed, including what she noticed about how she engaged the students during the session. The observer then shares his observation—what he saw, heard, and made note of. This sharing is followed by talk between the two colleagues about what did and did not occur related to the focusing question and what the observed teacher might do the next time. The session ends with the observing and the observed teachers reflecting on the process and what they learned as a result of it.

Support for Peer Observation

The leadership team at Parker Middle School knew there were some teachers in the school who were eager to have colleagues observe in their classrooms to give them feedback about their practice, and others who were not ready to do so. So, while some teachers were engaged in the *First Classroom Visits*

> Eventually people came to understand that the sole motive [for the observations] was to improve our practice.
> —Cathy O'Connell, Assistant Principal, Parker Middle School, Reading, Massachusetts

process, others joined a voluntary group facilitated by Cathy, the assistant principal, dedicated to observing and giving focused feedback. Members of this group participated in rounds of observations—sometimes as observers in a colleague's classroom and other times as the teacher being observed. Cathy reported that initially even these voluntarily involved faculty members were nervously hesitant to open their doors, but as the school continued to pursue practices that made sharing practice a regular and positive occurrence, they became more willing.

Both *First Classroom Visits* and the *Focus Point* protocol for peer observations are approaches that open classroom doors to colleagues. Both require school leaders to

1. Provide clarity as to how these visits inform or align with the instructional and curricular priorities of the school—and communicate those connections to everyone involved.
2. Set up the structures and monitor the needs and progress of the observation teams/partners throughout the process—answering questions, providing resources, and stepping in with assistance as needed.
3. Ensure that a discussion takes place among all the participating teachers during which they share perspectives, insights, and learning gained through their observations, and discuss implications for schoolwide practice.

The questions provided in Figure 3.3 can help a leader prepare for and support observations within a school, grade level, or content area.

CREATING LEARNING COMMUNITIES

In this section we consider learning communities as a strategy to support socializing learning. A learning community, or professional learning community, is a widely known and used concept and structure. In the context of socializing learning, a learning community is unique and stands in contrast to other groups operating in a school (e.g., study groups or committees). In

Figure 3.3. Preparing for and Supporting Observations among Colleagues

- What are the purposes of the visits and what procedures will be used? Will a standard form/template be used?
- How do teachers choose a focus for an observation?
- How are observations conducted and what notes should be taken?
- When are the pre-conferences, observations, and post-conferences to be held?
- How will observations be organized and coordinated? Will teachers choose observation partners or will the leader create matches based on practical issues (schedule, familiarity, etc.), readiness, expertise in instructional practice, or some combination?
- How will the leader check in on the observation teams or pairs to see what support or assistance they might need?
- When and how will the leader hold a group discussion with all participating teachers to share learning and discuss implications for practices across the grade level, content area, or school? What questions will guide that discussion? What processes will support it?

order to support socializing learning, we propose that a socializing learning community be made up of a small group (4–10) of educators who meet on a regular basis and over time to jointly learn, plan, inquire into, and solve problems related to teaching and learning.

Learning community members inquire into their practice, reflect on the results, and develop individual and collective action designed to improve their teaching and the learning of their students. It is through collaborative work done over time that the shift from the immediate, individualized focus of instrumental learning to the collaborative and reflective focus of socializing learning occurs (DuFour & Eaker, 1998; Lieberman & Miller, 2008; McLaughlin & Talbert, 2006). Kruse, Louis, and Bryk (1994) describe such communities as characterized by (1) collaboration, (2) reflection, (3) a focus

> We are not a learning community unless we are learning with and from one another. Sharing our practice. Learning. Changing. How do I act, think, and talk differently as a result?
>
> —Doug Lyons, Principal,
> Parker Middle School, Reading, Massachusetts

on issues of teaching and learning, (4) the de-privatization of practice, and (5) shared norms and values. These kinds of professional communities are able to make significant gains in student achievement (Lieberman & Miller, 2008; McLaughlin & Talbert, 2006; Newmann & Wehlage, 1995).

Purpose and Structure of Learning Communities

What will be the focus of the group's collaboration? What is the compelling work that can best be done in small groups? Richard DuFour and Robert Eaker (1998) put forth that the purpose of learning communities is to take on specific priorities or tasks identified by the school. Such was the focus of the learning communities created at Serna Elementary School, which created grade-level communities to support the implementation of locally developed mathematics assessments, a top instructional priority for the school.

Establishing a shared purpose and configuring the groups by grade levels permitted the Serna Elementary groups to focus on day-to-day instructional practices and their impact on the students in classrooms. Working in grade-level communities also helped to build ownership and accountability among the group members. It allowed members to come to agreement about their collective and individual actions within a familiar group. Having the teams organized by grade levels also made it easier to accomplish the logistics of arranging time to work in learning communities during the school day.

Teacher learning communities also might be used as an opportunity to build upon and expand knowledge and know-how gained from expert-based professional development (McLaughlin & Talbert, 2006). This was the starting place for Parker Middle School. Teachers participated in a variety of professional learning experiences related to integrating technology into their instructional practices. Learning communities were then formed to refine and expand those experiences by providing feedback on teacher practices and, eventually, to begin to create a coherent use of technology across the school.

Learning communities also might be configured around content or subject areas; for example, all of the high school foreign language teachers might form a group to focus on the implementation of a new curriculum. Groups also might be interdisciplinary, such as a middle school team with a focus on a shared group of students and how best to serve them. Perhaps a school has a particular schoolwide issue or dilemma, such as ensuring the success of second language learners, in which case a learning community might be established to study the issue and make recommendations to the school. Whatever their form, the learning communities are focused on important school priorities and are accountable to themselves and to the school to accomplish their work.

Initial Steps for Forming Learning Communities

Working in collaborative learning communities to share, plan, inquire, and take action is a significant shift away from the autonomous and often anonymous practice that characterizes most schools. Jeff Price, the principal of Serna Elementary School, knew that in order for these communities to be successful, they would need attention and structure. He and the leadership team carefully planned and prepared for their launch. During the first months of operation, a member of the leadership team facilitated each of the communities, ensuring that the groups had an opportunity to practice and learn the habits and skills needed to be successful.

Using a variety of protocols provided additional support for collaborative learning. The groups began by delving into the results of mathematics assessments that were developed by the school. The group identified implications for mathematics instruction and then devised classroom responses (lesson plans, teaching strategies, materials, etc.) to put in place. Results from the implementation of these efforts were brought back to the group for further reflection, thus establishing a cycle of recursive inquiry into the teaching and learning of mathematics across the school.

Working in a community with colleagues in this way can give teachers an opportunity to take learning from other professional development experiences, put it into practice, and reflect on its impact and implications with colleagues (McLaughlin & Talbert, 2006). Creating this type of bridge from more instrumental professional development that the teachers had experienced to the collaborative and reflective socializing learning of these learning communities was exactly what Jeff wanted to accomplish.

The following four reminders can help leaders as they design for learning communities:

- Set a focus on what matters—teaching and learning.
- Figure out group configurations, structures, and schedules.
- Incorporate protocols or other processes.
- Make connections across grade levels, content areas, and the school.

At Serna Elementary School, Jeff Price and the leadership team determined the purpose, focus, and configuration of the communities. They provided structure and support to ensure the success of the communities. Likewise, school leaders who are creating learning communities will need to determine, considering their own settings, the purpose and focus of their work, how the groups will be configured, and the support that is needed for them to be successful.

ENGAGING IN COLLABORATIVE SUPERVISION

Just as the manner in which teachers learn from and with one another shifts when they engage in socializing learning, so does the way in which a leader (whether a department or grade-level chair, instructional coach, principal, assistant principal, or other school leader) approaches supervision. As the experience, confidence, and skill of teachers as socializing learners develop, leaders also may adapt their supervisory practices.

When individuals and groups move into socializing learning and develop collaborative skills and experiences, the leader moves toward taking less control, engaging the teachers more in decision making, and shifting the responsibility for learning to the teachers (Glickman, Gordon, & Ross-Gordon, 2010). In this approach to collaborative supervision, the goal of supporting and encouraging long-term teacher development stays the same; it is the process that is different. The leader begins to practice behaviors that focus on helping teachers exercise their best thinking, planning, and action-taking (Kee, Anderson, Dearing, Harris, & Shuster, 2010). In collaborative supervision, the leader moves from the role of instructor to that of co-creator. The key is to move away from providing an answer toward arriving at a shared understanding of a goal, challenge, or issue, and a mutual agreement as to how to approach it. The leader shares her own point of view, but the focus is on encouraging the teacher to present his own perceptions and ideas, and then to co-develop learning plans. Drawing from a process developed by Glickman and colleagues (2010), a set of guiding questions can support a collaborative supervision conversation between a teacher and a supervisor (see Figure 3.4).

It is helpful to keep in mind the needs of socializing learners when moving toward a more collaborative approach to supervision. Socializing learners tend to place significant value on the opinion of those in a position of power or those whom they admire. They may not trust that the leader really wants to hear their point of view, or they may be reluctant to offer their perceptions, especially if they differ from those of the leader. It will be the role of the leader to consistently demonstrate a willingness and desire to be collaborative. The leader will need to practice good listening, exercise wait time, and resist jumping in with solutions or ideas.

SUPPORTING SOCIALIZING LEARNING:
IMPLICATIONS FOR LEADERSHIP

Socializing learning asks educators to move away from the focus of instrumental learning on individual's practices and toward multiple perspectives and shared understanding. Socializing learning requires educators to join

Figure 3.4. Guiding Questions for a Collaborative Supervision
    Conversation

- Clarifying the teacher's point of view: How does the teacher describe the
  goal or issue? What does the teacher think about the goal or issue?
- Checking in: Supervisor reflects back to the teacher what she heard —Am I
  understanding you correctly?
- Presenting the supervisor's point of view: How does the supervisor describe
  the goal or issue? What does the supervisor think about the goal or issue?
- Checking in: Teacher reflects back to the supervisor what he heard —Am I
  understanding you correctly?
- Creating next steps: Teacher and supervisor exchange possible approaches.
- Acknowledging different points of view: Where is there agreement? Where
  are there differences?
- Finding acceptable action: What do the agreements and differences suggest
  for a next step(s)?
- Agreeing on the details of the plan: What action will be taken and by whom?
  What resources are needed? Who will help? When?
- The conversation ends with the teacher and supervisor summarizing
  the final plan.

Adapted by the authors from C. D. Glickman, S. P. Gordon, & J. M. Ross-Gordon, 2010,
    pp.164–168.

with colleagues to collaborate with one another to examine, reflect on, and improve not only individual practice but also their collective practice.

Since schools are typically not reflective, collaborative places, it is the role of the leader to provide opportunity, strategies, skills, and dispositions that support socializing learning. Socializing learning requires that leaders not only provide teachers with opportunities to learn from and with their colleagues. It also requires leaders to play active roles promoting and engaging in socializing learning themselves, and to do so in public ways.

Modeling

Among the most powerful tools leaders have to support socializing learning is to model the strategies described in this chapter (and others) and incorporate them throughout their work. A leader might use protocols in whole-school and small-group meetings that the leader facilitates, thus offering everyone in the school an opportunity to practice these new processes and ways of thinking in an authentic way. A leader could facilitate one of the learning communities in the school, similar to the practice at Serna Elementary and Parker Middle School. The highly visible and consistent use of these processes by school leaders has the added benefit of underscoring that there is a new way to learn in place at the school, one that is valued and practiced by the school leadership. Emphasizing the debriefing and reflection phases of the protocols provides a chance to explore the benefits and challenges of using socializing protocols and practices and familiarizes everyone with facilitating them.

Being a Learner

A leader also might take up the learning he wants the teachers to undertake by seeking opportunities to put himself in the position of a learner. For example, he might select a piece of his own work he would like to improve and present it for feedback using a *Tuning* protocol. He might arrange for a colleague from another school to observe him facilitating a faculty meeting and give him feedback on some particular aspect of his leadership practice.

Providing Resources

Teachers are more likely to engage in collaborative learning with others when logistical barriers are removed. Assigning resources and coordinating logistics can be crucial. At both Serna Elementary and Parker Middle School, the leadership teams made certain that the teachers had the time, resources, and tools that they needed to work collaboratively. Doug, the principal, and Cathy, the assistant principal at Parker Middle School, established a pool of release time and coordinated classroom visits at the school. At Serna Elementary, grad-level teams were allotted common planning time that made collaborative work possible. Assigning resources to socializing learning strategies also signals the seriousness of the leadership's commitment to the endeavor.

Aligning Learning with Purpose

Finally, socializing learning lays the groundwork for the collaborative, reflective learning that is necessary to make substantive and sustainable changes in teaching and learning within a school. To bring the most coherence and power to these socializing learning practices, leaders need to ensure that the learning among the adults is aligned with the school's purpose of improving student learning and with its instructional priorities (Glickman, 2002).

Challenges for Leaders

A significant challenge of realizing socializing learning lies in the shift that it represents from the way schools typically operate. Socializing learning requires the leader to remain steadfast and committed to this new way of learning, especially in the face of resistance and pressure to return to the more familiar. Cathy recounted that some Parker Middle School teachers initially greeted protocols and learning communities with skepticism. What's a protocol? What's this jargon? What's a learning community? When they instituted classroom observations, some teachers wanted to know what the assignment was. What are we supposed to learn or do as a result? There was no assignment, other than to begin a different kind of conversation. Eventually, after multiple protocol experiences, and after rounds of class-room visits, the conversation began to change. The teachers began asking questions and inquiring into their own and others' practices, eager to learn from and with their colleagues.

The leader putting in place these strategies in support of socializing learning also must consider the levels of safety and risk that are perceived by the participants. These perceptions will be unique to each individual. What might be considered challenging but safe for one teacher—It feels risky to ask for help to improve my lesson plan, but I know that I'll receive feedback that will be helpful—may be full of danger for another—I couldn't ask my colleagues for feedback, what might they think of me? Each strategy and each group or individual will require the leader to provide sufficient scaf-folding to ensure that each teacher feels safe enough to take the risks needed for new learning. The leader's role is to anticipate and plan for these needs.

When instrumental learners are asked to move their focus from immediate, personal concerns to larger issues of teaching and learning, they need specific support for that shift. These teachers are rightfully wor-ried about their daily classroom practice. Acknowledging their concerns and providing the direction and instruction they need are key. And, at the same time, a leader must urge them to explore other possibilities. For example, a leader might give teachers the opportunity to observe col-leagues who teach differently than they do, to both expand their teach-ing repertoire and develop an awareness of a range of effective teaching strategies and practices. In processes that invite and require everyone to offer feedback on ideas or a collaborative plan, the leader might begin by having teachers work with one or two trusted colleagues before sharing with or contributing to the larger group.

For socializing learners, thoughtful implementation of these strategies is essential. Starting with lower stakes processes such as a text protocol is a strategy that will help build confidence and familiarity in participating in a collaborative discussion with colleagues guided by a protocol. Both Parker Middle School and Serna Elementary initially engaged in multiple experi-ences of reading and responding to text using protocols prior to trying out other types of collaborative learning. Additionally, they created norms that established the ways group members would aspire to act when engaged in collaborative learning.

Likewise, first efforts at Parker Middle School to formally share prac-tice were set up to take into account a range of readiness that existed among the faculty members. Opportunities were organized for teachers who were ready to experience the challenge of opening their practice to observers with feedback, while those who were just beginning to explore collaborative learning could be engaged as observers and learners in initial visits.

Leaders who are building their school's capacity for socializing learning are also challenged to find ways to support self-authoring learners. Parker Middle School addressed this issue by identifying teachers who were ready for other challenging learning. These teachers participated in multiple pro-fessional learning sessions dedicated to the facilitation of learning communi-ties and the skillful use of protocols. Doug and Cathy also arranged for these same teachers to participate in national conferences that brought together educators from across the country who are engaged in this type of collab-orative, socializing learning. These teacher-leaders became members of the school's instructional leadership team, facilitating protocols and leading professional development sessions. Their own development was enhanced as they took on new roles and responsibilities across the school.

Socializing learning lays the groundwork for the creation of a school as a vibrant learning community, one in which the school begins to make public previously held private practices and in which teachers begin to learn from one another. The focus of the learning moves beyond an individual teacher improving her own practice in her individual setting toward the learning of the group.

However, socializing learning is limited by its need for "agreement" in which an individual's point of view may be set aside if it conflicts with oth-ers in the group. Significant issues related to teaching and learning might be avoided because they are discomforting or require difficult conversations.

The next step in building capacity for adult learning in schools is to put in place supports and strategies so that differences of opinion are seen as sources of learning, not something to be avoided. While there are many times when consensus is a desirable outcome, the next phase of learning requires a more critical inquiry approach. The locus of attention, which shifted from the individual in instrumental learning to the collaborative group in socializing learning, shifts again in self-authoring learning toward broader community capacity and responsibility.

CHAPTER 4

Self-Authoring Learning in Schools

These conversations are so tough. Here I am, a Black woman with a set of whole new ideas, standing up in front of mostly White people.

—Addie Hawkins, former Director of Equity, Kansas City, Kansas, School District

As educators and the schools in which they work develop capacity for learning, they begin to wonder about practices typically taken for granted: How many students didn't earn credit for algebra because they didn't complete homework? How many of those students otherwise would have passed? They question the assumptions about students, teaching, and learning that are embedded in those practices. What does this say about what we believe is important about being a successful learner? They want to not only improve practice but also question those practices. In these schools, educators are ready to take on the challenging work of self-authoring learning.

In this chapter we offer various approaches to self-authoring learning that allow educators to engage in sustained thoughtful examination of assumptions about and purposes of teaching and learning. These approaches help educators to "learn more about their own, and each other's, most deeply held attitudes and beliefs" and to take action based on this new learning (Senge et al., 2000, p. 68).

PLANNING FOR SELF-AUTHORING LEARNING

Self-authoring learning is rare for both individuals and schools. It stands in stark contrast to the increasing pressure on today's schools and school leaders for immediate, decisive, and short-term solutions to problems.

Schools have always felt the urgency of addressing the learning, social, psychological, and even physical needs of the hundreds of students who enter their doors every day. Schools now experience not only that pressure, but also the demand to raise achievement in ways that can be measured by standardized tests and statistical analysis (Darling-Hammond, 2010; Glickman, 1993; Senge et al., 2000). Self-authoring learning, however, requires work that is much different; it asks schools and school leaders to make time and space to publicly raise and dig into challenging questions that resist easy answers. A self-authoring school is one that invests in the long-term transformation of schooling in the service of the learning of each one of its students.

School leaders who engage themselves and their schools in self-authoring learning use various strategies to slow down and interrogate typical and comfortable patterns of thinking so that everyone becomes more aware of their individual and the school's collective mental models. Taking on this type of learning increases anxiety as disquieting questions are raised and ambiguity replaces the certainty of best practices. It is, therefore, not enough for leaders to encourage or support these strategies—they must be at the center of them, engaging in the asking and learning. In order for others to know that it is safe to take the risks that self-authoring learning and school transformation require, a leader must become the lead learner and risk taker. Self-authoring learning raises the stakes of what it means to be a successful school and a successful school leader.

UNIQUENESS OF SELF-AUTHORING LEARNING

Many of the strategies and structures offered in this chapter and throughout this book can provide powerful learning opportunities for educators and schools at every place along the developmental arc. They all require the support and engagement of school leaders, benefit from skillful facilitation, need a clear purpose or focusing question, and call for some degree of risk taking by participants, and many make use of protocols or agreed-upon processes or structures. What distinguishes them, or makes them appropriate for different learners and different schools, is their focus and purpose.

How does a leader ensure that an approach will push the learning of a school from socializing to self-authoring? How does a leader use an approach to increase understanding of a school's collective mental models? We believe there are two unique qualities of self-authoring learning in schools that distinguish it from socializing learning: (1) a focus on previously undiscussable issues and (2) the persistent pursuit of challenging questions. Being aware of these differences will help leaders guide the development of their schools toward the transformative work of self-authoring learning.

Discussing the Undiscussable

Rather than seeking a best practice as an instrumental learning school might, or agreement and coherence in practice that a socializing learning school might, a self-authoring school seeks to raise questions that will push the practice of its teachers and leaders beyond the current boundaries of their traditions, assumptions, and beliefs. Leaders in these schools mobilize people to tackle tough problems. This means not only seeking better ways of working on behalf of students, but also trying to understand and make meaning of what is happening in terms of the teaching and learning within the school.

Through this questioning, issues are raised that previously might have been "undiscussable" (Argyris, 1982). These undiscussables may be those things that are taken for granted and, therefore, hidden from view, even to the people who are in the school (Schein, 2010). They may be issues and topics that schools do not know whether or how to talk about, such as those connected to privilege and power, including the influence of race, gender, socioeconomic status, nationality, ethnicity, language, and sexuality. Such undiscussable issues "tend to be about the uncomfortable, unequal, ineffective, prejudicial conditions and relationships in a school" (Eubanks, Parish, & Smith, 1997, p. 155). It is important for a leader to know that when undiscussables are brought into the open and examined, the ensuing discussion may be considered dangerous. The danger arises from questioning the values and beliefs operating within the school, which can result in members of the school feeling threatened (Heifetz et al., 2009).

A story shared by a Latina colleague about her experience posing a question related to race illustrates the risky and difficult nature of undiscussable topics in many schools. Her question was raised as the focus of a professional dilemma that she brought to her colleagues for feedback on, using a *Consultancy* protocol led by external facilitators (see Appendix C for the *Consultancy* description).

> I said I had a dilemma I could bring to the group that was authentic, but it might be a little risky. I had been waiting for a long time to talk about race at [our high school]. [Our school] was at that time, and I contend still is now, a school in denial. I remember the district not wanting us to start a mariachi group because we didn't want to be "too Mexican." The teachers were mourning the loss of a largely White, middle- to upper-middle-class student population. The face of [our school] had changed but we avoided saying the words *Hispanic*, *Mexican*, or *Latino*. What I hated, what really wounded me, was that our Latino kids did not feel like they were part of the school— they were outsiders despite the fact that they were the majority

> One teacher was completely offended that we would "talk about this" and "bring race into it." I remember that she also wrote about this in her reflections for the day. I can't remember much else except that it was awkward and painful.
>
> —A Latina colleague

numerically. With encouragement and coaching of our facilitators, I crafted a question: How can I encourage my Latino students to take on leadership roles in Latin club? It doesn't sound like much. During the protocol, I remember things going pretty well, although some people didn't say much. The debrief, however, was tough. One teacher was completely offended that we would "talk about this" and "bring race into it." I remember that she also wrote about this in her reflections for the day. I can't remember much else except that it was awkward and painful. Did presenting the dilemma make a difference? I'm not sure. But at least people knew where I was coming from.

Although our colleague's question might not, as she describes it, "sound like much," it was enough to trigger strong responses. The question raised the issue of race and how it influenced practices in the school. For both educators, the question held danger because it challenged the assumptions, beliefs, and practices that guided the way the school operated.

These types of challenging questions and the ensuing dialogue provide the second defining characteristic of self-authoring learning.

Challenging Questions and Dialogue
About Assumptions and Purposes

Self-authoring learning expands the scope of a school's learning beyond the implementation of programs, curriculum, strategies, and structures. This means that school leaders and other members of a school's faculty do more than raise questions about how a program is put into action or the results of implementing it. They also consider why it is a part of the practice of their school. Who benefits from it? What does a particular program say about our beliefs about students, teaching and learning, and the purpose of schooling? Does it make a difference for each of our students, or does it simply offer the semblance of change that eventually will lead to the same results, the same students failing, and the same students succeeding? (For more questions that self-authoring schools might ask, see Figure 4.1.)

Figure 4.1. Questions That Self-Authoring Schools Might Ask

- Why are we assigning homework? Does it improve or expand understanding or skills? What would happen if we no longer required homework? Who benefits from homework? Who does not?
- What difference does it make that most of our faculty members are White and most of our students are African American or Latino? What is the impact of our racial make-up on the school experience of our students, especially our students of color? What do we need to do about that?
- How does the importance of external, standardized measures to determine success influence the school experience of our students who struggle the most?
- Why are the most engaging, active learning experiences available only to students who have been the most successful in traditional schooling? What does that practice say about our assumptions about our students? What would happen if we involved everyone in these kinds of experiences?

Senge and his colleagues (2000) describe these types of questions and subsequent conversations as dialogue—a discussion where people can become more aware of the context around their experiences and what led to the creation of that context. "Dialogue then serves to encourage people to suspend their assumptions . . . [by] bringing them forward, making them explicit, giving them considerable 'weight,' and trying to figure out where they come from" (pp. 75–76). It is through dialogue focused on challenging questions about previously undiscussable issues that a school begins the journey toward transformational change.

APPROACHES TO SELF-AUTHORING LEARNING

When schools engage in discussion around issues of teaching and learning, the conversation frequently is focused on implementing a new program, curriculum, or instructional strategy. After implementation, the school's attention may turn to creating alignment and coherence across a grade level, content area, or school. When ideas or strategies emerge that are in conflict with the current practice of some (or all) of the educators, a discussion of the beliefs that underlie those practices might arise. In these discussions, educators may defend current practices, try to convince others to change, or seek a compromise that will resolve the conflict and allow them to get back to work.

How can leaders support the kind of self-authoring dialogue that would allow educators to engage in sustained, thoughtful examination of assumptions and the purposes of teaching and learning? The following approaches

> There may be only paths to discover, not answers.
>
> Eubanks, Parish, and Smith, 1997, p. 157

have the potential to "permit teachers to make visible their understanding and practices of classroom teaching and to learn, interrupt, problematize, or reinvent those practices" with one another (Little, 2003, p. 920).

The first approach is about engaging in dialogue about issues of equity and educational excellence. There are many lenses through which a school can consider equity; these include race, ethnicity, gender, language, sexuality, and socioeconomic status. We focus specifically on race because it is a persistent and powerful determinant of student success in many schools and a topic that is often undiscussable. We then describe teacher-led inquiry, lesson study, and critical friends groups as three more approaches for self-authoring learning.

As we begin these descriptions, leaders need to keep in mind that in self-authoring learning there are no easy answers or solutions and no simple approach or strategy to put in place. Rather, it is the engagement in the asking, the continuous seeking, and rigorous examination of action that will move schools toward transformation.

LEARNING ABOUT RACE AND EQUITY

How do leaders engage in, lead, and support dialogue about the racial achievement gap and other issues of race, racism, and equity that exist in most schools? Addie Hawkins, then-Director of Equity in the Kansas City, Kansas, School District, undertook a multiple-year journey engaging her school district in such a dialogue. She was charged by the superintendent to work to close the achievement gap between African American and other students of color and their White counterparts.

Addie subscribed to Singleton and Linton's (2006) assertion that educators can't talk about disparities in racial achievement "without first learning how to effectively talk about race" (p. 229). *Courageous Conversations About Race* (Singleton & Linton, 2006) became the cornerstone of the Kansas City school district's effort to address the racial achievement gap. This approach brings a rigor to the enterprise of taking on issues of equity. It not only sets forth a set of agreements and understandings, but also offers guiding questions and processes to ensure sharply focused attention on issues of race, racism, and equity.

Agreements to Support Conversations About Race

In the framework outlined in *Courageous Conversations About Race* (2006, 2007), Singleton and Linton put forth a set of agreements designed specifically to support conversations about race. Such agreements can help create space in which educators engage in conversations they otherwise might not even attempt (see Chapter 5 for further discussion of agreements). In the case of self-authoring learning, educators are called upon to commit to engaging in challenging and difficult conversations or dialogue specifically about race. Commitment and adherence to these agreements can provide safety and create the conditions that enable educators to engage in dialogue about race in which they are deeply invested. Such agreements are critical in order for self-authoring learners to have the space and conditions so that they can hear, analyze, and incorporate the points of view of others into their own mental models. These agreements include:

Stay engaged. Each person commits to remaining emotionally and intellectually involved, including when the conversation becomes difficult.

Speak your truth. This agreement offers an invitation to take the risk of being honest about feelings, thoughts, and opinions.

Experience discomfort. As schools engage in examining the previously undiscussable beliefs and assumptions about race, personal and collective discomfort is to be expected. This agreement acknowledges that discomfort is necessary for real change to occur.

Expect and accept nonclosure. Engaging in dialogue about race is not a search for the best practice to close the racial gap in schools. It is, like all of self-authoring learning, a way to examine a complex issue and requires nonclosure, a tolerance for ambiguity, and ongoing inquiry.

A more extensive discussion of these agreements to support complex and challenging conversations about race can be found in *Courageous Conversations About Race* (Singleton & Linton, 2006, pp. 53–67). These agreements define *how* a group has a conversation. However, dialogue about race requires attending to not only the "how" question but also the content of the conversations. What is the content of these courageous conversations?

Processes and Content to Support Conversations About Race

Based on their work with educators, Singleton and Linton (2006, 2007) identify six conditions for the content and processes necessary for courageous conversations about race. These conditions build upon one another and become progressively more challenging. Together they provide the basis for creating new shared values, beliefs, and actions that can lead to transforming schools. The following brief descriptions draw from the more extensive treatment of these complex issues by Singleton and Linton (2006, 2007).

Establishing a racial context that is personal, local, and immediate. Courageous conversations about race begin by exploring personal racial attitudes, beliefs, and expectations. An initial focus on personal experiences can increase educators' awareness of race and how it impacts their school and the experiences of their students.

Isolating race. Conversations remain explicitly and intentionally focused on race. Steadfastly focusing on race can counter the tendency of a group to retreat to less challenging and more familiar topics, such as poverty, when they become uncomfortable.

Engaging multiple racial perspectives. This condition recognizes that individuals from different racial groups will have different points of view about race. Seeking to understand the perspectives of persons of color can begin to build better understandings of how racism is experienced and the impact it has. By acknowledging the normality of multiple racial points of view and embracing these differences, educators can find "new ways of looking at the challenges of effectively educating all children" (Singleton & Linton, 2007, p. 109).

Keeping us all at the table. As the group develops an understanding of why these courageous conversations are so difficult, members become better able to create the safety needed to take risks in speaking the truth of their own experiences. The group actively manages its conversations to ensure effective dialogue by using techniques that support multiple points of view, maintain focus through the use of specific and explicit prompts, and provide sufficient time for everyone to feel "listened to and validated" (Singleton & Linton, 2007, p. 134).

What do you mean by "race"? In the fifth condition, educators are guided to create a working definition of race by exploring the history of race and examining its impact on schools. This definition distinguishes among race, ethnicity, and nationality to underscore the power of race in defining an individual in our culture and to ensure that the conversation remains focused on race.

Let's talk about Whiteness. This final condition explores the racial dominance of Whiteness, how it impacts conversations about race, and how it influences teaching and learning. This condition asks group members to raise questions about what it means to be White and how Whiteness impacts daily experiences, schooling, and the success of students.

> It is my job as the instructional leader to fight for the equity issues.
> —Michael Cardona, Principal,
> Lee High School, San Antonio, Texas

By engaging in courageous conversations, leaders can support self-authoring learning. In this structured forum, educators can explore their own mental models of race and to come to know the perspectives of others. Through this ongoing dialogue and examination, a school can come to develop a more critical lens through which to examine and assess its practices, beliefs, and attitudes. As our colleague Addie discovered, Singleton and Linton's *Courageous Conversations About Race* (2006, 2007) offers leaders both a process and content to engage their schools in dialogue about undiscussable beliefs, attitudes, assumptions, and practices related to race and racism that can lead to the transformation of practice.

INQUIRING INTO PRACTICE

Although it might be tempting to consider teacher-led inquiry as "a natural extension of good teaching" (Hubbard & Power, 1999, p. 3), it requires the development of an intentional and disciplined practice. Teacher-led research calls for a "purposeful research attitude . . . something beyond the reflective moment, a line of thought to be pursued in a passionate and integrated manner" (Bisplinghoff & Allen, 1998, p. 7). It is this passionate engagement, supported by the rigor of a research process, that can lead to the transformation of individual and school practices.

In teacher-led inquiry, a teacher or group of teachers identify a compelling question about their practice, investigate it by capturing evidence from and about their school settings, examine that evidence from different points of view, reflect on its implications, and revise their actions and subsequent questions in light of their discussions and experiences (Weinbaum, Allen, Blythe, Simon, Seidel, & Rubin, 2004). Teacher-led inquiry goes below the surface and often challenges the reliance on external standardized test scores to evaluate student learning and the rush to adopt best practices from other settings to address any shortcomings. Rather, inquiry encourages teachers to investigate their own experience and knowledge within the specific context of their classrooms.

Inquiry Process

Although it incorporates a series of processes, teacher-led inquiry is not linear. Teachers may begin by identifying a focusing or framing question or some aspect of their practice to explore; however, as they begin to investigate, their focus often shifts as they gain insight and come to understand the multiple layers or complexity of the issues.

One step is not completed before another begins, and the steps might be taken in a different order, depending on the teacher, the question, the context, the data, and the findings. The process might be better imagined as recursive rather than linear. A teacher might enter at any point and move through the various aspects of the process in any order.

The evidence process diagram developed by Project Zero at Harvard's Graduate School of Education (Figure 4.2) offers an overview of the process of teacher-led inquiry and how the pieces of the process are related to one another (as cited in Weinbaum et al., 2004, p. 48). Teachers might begin by forming questions and then move to gathering evidence (student work samples, journal entries, observational notes, interviews, etc.). They continue by making sense of the data, perhaps by discussing them with others or analyzing them using a protocol with colleagues as they move through the process. The gears analogy in this figure highlights the interconnectedness of the various aspects of the process and the multiple entry points into it.

Inquiry as a Stance

Teacher-led inquiry becomes self-authoring when inquiry is regarded as a "stance rather than as project or strategy" (Cochran-Smith, 2002, p. 9). It is this shift toward unearthing the underlying assumptions and investigating multiple points of view that makes teacher-led inquiry self-authoring.

The questions put forth by educators who have been engaged in inquiry for a number of years illustrate this stance toward their practice. For example:

- How can I make each ELL (English language learner) student's story visible in the culture of my classroom, and what happens to student learning when I do so? (Mindy Paulo, English Language Learner Curriculum Coordinator, Brookline Public Schools, Massachusetts)
- What aspects of the school do families of color experience as supportive and effective, and how can we build on what works for my classroom? (Annie Leonard, Assistant High School Principal, Amherst Regional High School, Massachusetts)

Figure 4.2. The Evidence Process ("Gears" Diagram)

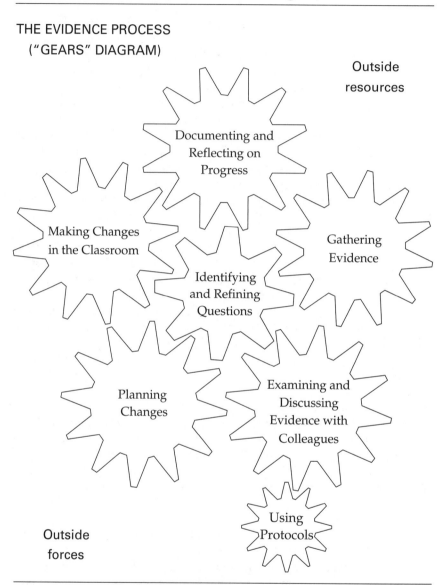

THE EVIDENCE PROCESS
("GEARS" DIAGRAM)

Outside
resources

Documenting and
Reflecting on
Progress

Making Changes
in the Classroom

Gathering
Evidence

Identifying
and Refining
Questions

Planning
Changes

Examining and
Discussing
Evidence with
Colleagues

Using
Protocols

Outside
forces

From *Teaching as Inquiry: Asking Hard Questions to Improve Practice and Student Achievement*, by A. Weinbaum, D. Allen, T. Blythe, K. Simon, S. Seidel, and C. Rubin, 2004, New York: Teachers College Press. Reprinted with permission from Steve Seidel at Project Zero.

Unearthing Assumptions

- What do we see in the data?
- Are we just seeing what we expect to see?
- Who might see the data differently?
- What are we willing to give up or change as a result?

As teacher-researcher Sally Bryan observed, "If [my students] are unable to do something, instead of saying, 'Well, you got that wrong,' you say, 'Now wait a minute, what is going on here that this child didn't get it? Did I not teach this well?' Obviously I have to revisit it" (Mohr, Rogers, Sanford, Nocerino, MacLean, & Clawson, 2004, p. 78).

A school might begin its self-authoring inquiry by investigating a troubling achievement gap, or by looking at instructional challenges within a particular grade level or content area.

Through its inquiry, a school can begin to claim shared responsibility for the success of each student and the knowledge and skill to realize that success. When leaders support and promote context-specific inquiry into the assumptions and beliefs surrounding teaching and learning, schools can move from a dependence on external measures of success to "produce precisely the kind of knowledge" needed by the school to educate all of its students well (Lytle & Cochran-Smith, 1992, p. 466).

Schools engaging in teacher-led inquiry can benefit from the support of external resources to provide experience, knowledge, skills, and even facilitation of the process. Additional information about teacher-led inquiry, including examples of ongoing inquiry initiatives, can be found in Appendix F (Resources).

We have to develop the capacity to identify and explicitly work on the questions that matter most to our students—the questions or aspects of our practice that perhaps make us the most uncomfortable.
—Thompson-Grove, 2008, p. viii

ENGAGING IN LESSON STUDY

Schools frequently have in place some type of lesson-planning process, along with time for teachers to regularly plan daily, weekly, or unit-based lessons with colleagues. Such planning is encouraged, perhaps even required, as a method to improve teaching and align instruction and curriculum. Lesson planning often follows a format that may include: (1) stating the purpose, standards, or objectives of a lesson; (2) identifying the teaching methods, strategies, and materials; and (3) describing the evaluation or assessment processes. This kind of process may result in more focused planning, improved curricular and instructional alignment, and greater accountability. However, it is not designed as an opportunity to raise challenging questions about teaching and learning. How might leaders use lesson planning as a path to self-authoring learning?

Lesson study is a particular approach to planning for teaching that integrates planning, peer observation, and inquiry to create a powerful professional learning tool. Adopted from Japanese educators for use in the United States, lesson study brings a rigor and focus to the planning process that shifts it toward being a self-authoring endeavor.

In lesson study, educators collaboratively examine, question, and refine their individual and collective mental models of teaching. Lesson study accommodates teachers with different understandings about content and differences in experience and knowledge. It can grow to accommodate the learning of the group members engaged in the process (Lewis, Perry, Foster, Hurd, & Fisher, 2011). The process engages teachers in dialogue about teaching and learning through the focus on a particular lesson. The structure of lesson study is essential to create the conditions for self-authoring learning. It supports teachers so they can take on the challenging work of questioning their own and their colleagues' beliefs, assumptions, and practices related to teaching and learning.

The lesson study process includes five essential elements. The following brief description offers leaders an overview of the process, an understanding of the learning potential embedded in the process, and the kinds of support

> We usually plan with people we are comfortable with because they teach in a similar way. In lesson study, planning becomes more dynamic and honest since there is the expectation that everyone will teach the lesson in a similar way. It helps raise up who thinks differently and why.
>
> —Cathy O'Connell, Assistant Principal,
> Parker Middle School, Reading, Massachusetts

that a school or group of teachers might require in order to set up this learning. This overview is based on the work of Catherine Lewis and the Lesson Study Group at Mills College (Lesson Study Group at Mills College, 2011; Lewis, Perry, & Hurd, 2004, 2009).

Establish a Research Theme or Focus

Teachers working in small groups set a long-term theme that addresses both academic and social purposes of learning. Establishing a theme requires teachers to articulate and question the beliefs and assumptions they individually and collectively hold related to the purpose of education, the students they teach, and their roles as teachers. For example, a group of science teachers might ask, "What is important that students understand about climate?" whereas literacy teachers might wonder, "What makes poetry so difficult for our students?" Or, teachers might ask, "What are the learning characteristics we desire for all of our students? What are the actual learning characteristics of our students now? What are the implications of this gap for our teaching?"

Determine the Lesson Content

In addition to the research theme, teachers carefully select a specific content area for focus. They study the content to identify key concepts and standards to be included in the lesson and anticipate their students' learning.

Plan the Lesson

Working as a collaborative group, teachers create a lesson (or a unit of multiple lessons) that brings to life their long-term vision of education, specific academic content, and their students' needs. The development of the lesson asks the teachers to deepen their knowledge of the content they will be teaching, share and expand their instructional expertise, and plan how they will collect data about the lesson.

> Observing the lesson from the vantage of the students' experiences offers teachers a unique opportunity to gain new insight about the impact of the lesson on the students' engagement and learning.
> —Cathy O'Connell, Assistant Principal,
> Parker Middle School, Reading, Massachusetts

Research the Lesson

The lesson is taught by one of the members of the lesson-planning group; the others observe and gather evidence related to student learning and development. The observation focuses on the social and academic goals the group established, not on the teacher and her individual practice.

Reflect on the Lesson

Following the lesson, the group gathers to reflect on it and examine the data collected. The focus of the reflection and feedback is on the lesson, with an eye toward the redesign of this lesson and future ones. The process does not end with the redesign, but rather continues as the group members consider the implications for their growing understanding of teaching and learning and their students.

Through this type of ongoing dialogue, leaders can engage their schools in a planning process that supports self-authoring learning. Although not every lesson is developed using this approach, lesson study offers a forum for teachers to raise challenging questions about the assumptions and purposes of schooling as well as specific content and teaching. Lesson study provides a structure that can help teachers reveal, question, and expand their own mental models of teaching and learning and come to know and learn from the points of views of others. These insights and expanded understandings can add up to a shift in the way that teaching and learning are carried out in a school.

CRITICAL FRIENDS GROUPS

Many schools have put in place some form of a professional learning community in which educators work collaboratively to reflect on their practice, examine evidence of its impact, and make changes to improve teaching and learning. However, the work of self-authoring learning requires discipline, courage, and persistence, which are not always found within learning communities as they operate in many schools (DuFour, 2011). A critical friends group (CFG) is a particular form of learning community designed to provide the focus and structure needed to support self-authoring learning (Annenberg Institute for School Reform, 1997; School Reform Initiative, 2012a).

Like many of the other approaches described in this text, critical friends groups might be used to support educators at every place along the learning arc. For instrumental learners, a group might help them learn new strategies or implement new curriculum. For socializing learners, the learning might be focused on improving practice by receiving feedback on lesson plans, aligning curriculum, or developing common assessments.

When I first started in the CFG, I thought leadership was like being a fireman. There is a fire, and I will dump water on it and put it out. I learned sometimes the fire is a grease fire, and you should not put water on it or sometimes the fire is useful. [My CFG] has allowed me to say I don't know. To look at things in lots of ways, to see the many layers that there are. I don't think I was always that way. I thought I had to have the answer.

—Wayne Clark, Principal,
Shamrock Elementary, Woburn, Massachusetts

In the context of self-authoring learning, critical friends groups offer a forum in which members challenge deep-seated assumptions about teaching and learning, gain different perspectives about their students, surface troubling issues of equity in schools, and take up questions connected to the purpose of school. Learning within a CFG can help participants question how they know what they know, be emotionally open to exposing fundamental assumptions, and surface ideas that they have accepted uncritically in the past. CFGs can support and sustain self-authoring learning.

Critical friends groups have distinctive characteristics that make it more likely that learning in a community will build the capacity for self-authoring learning.

Critical Friends Groups Are Voluntary and Sustained

A critical friends group is made up of six to ten educators who meet regularly, typically every 4 to 6 weeks, over a sustained period of time. Membership is frequently voluntary (although there are successful exceptions). Voluntary participation helps to increase the likelihood that the members are committed to taking on risky and challenging work and staying engaged over time. Similarly, CFGs continue to work together beyond the completion of a time cycle such as a semester or school year. A leader who supports such a group signals that school transformation requires sustained, persistent work over time.

Critical Friends Groups Require Skilled Facilitation and the Discipline of Protocols

A skilled and experienced facilitator, frequently a participating member, supports the learning of a critical friends group (see Chapter 5 for a discussion of the role of a facilitator). Among the roles of a CFG facilitator are to

> I look at our CFG as having rigor. There is always a focus. People bring a problem. We use a protocol.
>
> —Liz Matthews, Principal,
> Highlands Elementary School, Danvers, Massachusetts

(1) develop and use norms and agreements to support the group's collaborative examination of private practice, (2) help the group members reflect upon their learning around teaching and learning as well as what it means to build a learning community, and (3) support the use of protocols.

As a group develops, the facilitator may not facilitate every meeting or protocol experience but rather focus on building the group's capacity for learning. One way a group builds its learning capacity is through the use of protocols. The group relies on the discipline of protocols to sustain its steadfast focus on teaching and learning. Protocols also offer the structure that allows a group to practice the skills and assume the dispositions of self-authoring learning. The more rigorous and facile the group becomes in the use of protocols and the more skillful the facilitation, the better able the group is to dig into challenging questions and issues.

How Critical Friends Groups Work

A critical friends group's meeting usually is structured around one or two issues of practice brought to the group by its members. Prior to a group meeting, the member who is presenting an issue holds a pre-conference with the facilitator to select a protocol that will provide the most helpful feedback. In the following section we describe what occurred in one CFG when a member brought a professional dilemma to the group for feedback. In keeping with the challenge posed earlier in this chapter for leaders to become the lead learners and risk takers in their schools, we are presenting the efforts of a CFG group of leaders who have taken up this charge.

> [Our CFG is] where you learn with other principals and don't have to fake it—pretend to know the answer when you don't.
>
> —Rubén Carmona, Principal,
> Lincoln Elementary School, Lowell, Massachusetts

The Tri-District Initiative in Leadership Education (TILE) is a critical friends group sponsored by Salem State University in Salem, Massachusetts. It is made up of school leaders—principals, assistant principals, and district office personnel (Fahey, 2011). The work of this 8-year-old group illustrates the potential for a long-standing CFG group to engage in self-authoring learning.

The group is voluntary. There are no state or district mandates and no assigned tasks that compel this group of leaders to learn together. They gather as a CFG because it is a place where they can take on difficult aspects of their work as leaders. This CFG allows them to step outside their hectic, fragmented daily professional lives to examine and question issues and questions related to their practice. As one member shared, "[Our CFG is] a critical reminder about what our real work is."

The TILE CFG collaborates to support its members in deprivatizing their practice and exploring difficult issues that may be high-stakes, and even undiscussable, in their individual settings. Such was the case when Clarke, one of the members of the TILE group, brought a dilemma to the group related to school culture. The following is a summary of the ensuing dialogue in which the group both challenged and supported the presenter to examine his own assumptions and explore other perspectives. (All names in the following section are pseudonyms.)

The group used a *Consultancy* protocol, facilitated by Sara, who had experience facilitating protocols. The purpose of the protocol, as Sara explained, was to help Clarke gain a different perspective on his dilemma, not to identify a single solution. In first phase of the protocol, Clarke presented an overview of his dilemma. He opened with the posing of a question—How important is a good culture in a school? — and proceeded to describe a culture of complaint and unhappiness among the staff at his school that he found personally draining and a detriment to learning. He gave examples of how teachers continually threatened to go to the union, complained about one another, criticized parents, disparaged the central office, and grumbled about his leadership. He eventually revealed, "I sometimes reach the end of my rope and I get kind of sad when I have to deal with this all the time." At the end of his presentation, when Sara prompted Clarke to restate his focusing question, he asked: "So, how important is a good culture in school when academics are pretty good and the kids love their school experience? Maybe I should just concentrate on the parents, work with parents, and set things up that way because there's enough work there to keep me busy."

Following the protocol, the group initially worked to better understand Clarke's dilemma by asking clarifying questions about the context, such as the number of staff who lived in the district, the role of teacher aides, and the grade levels of the most negative staff. Sara then moved the group to the next phase of the protocol by asking, "Are there probing questions—these are wondering questions, what-if questions, why, and what-were-you-thinking-when questions?"

Rather than moving into solving Clarke's dilemma, the group slowed down to ensure they were building a clear, shared understanding. Responding to these questions about his dilemma required Clarke to dig deeper, be reflective, question his assumptions, and consider a variety of possibilities.

The group probed Clarke's relationship with the central administration, the other principals, allies in the building, and defining moments in his principalship. They delved into the nature of the school and its culture. For example, building on a series of probing questions, Ellen asked Clarke, "Do you think the staff perceives you as off kilter because of this persistent culture of complaint? Do you feel off kilter?" Clarke paused and then responded, "I feel that they've got me dancing like a little puppet." He went on to share that he was feeling defensive and distracted by the pervasive complaining. The culture of complaint was keeping him from concentrating on the work he knew the school needed to do and he wanted to lead.

The group also pushed back on Clarke's initial question, which seemed to assume that a school leader could ignore school culture and focus on other work. The group challenged him to consider that it is the role of the leader to take up the work of creating a positive school culture.

Sara moved the group from probing questions to the discussion phase of the protocol. With Clarke listening in and taking notes, the group members reflected on what they had heard, what they considered the issues to be, and what different perspectives might exist. For example, they agreed that the problem was deeply rooted, probably as a result of long-standing hiring practices of past principals and the way in which new teachers had been inducted into the school culture. They also agreed that the school's strong performance on standardized tests took away a sense of urgency to address issues of school culture. They then began to discuss the importance of school culture and its connection to teaching and learning. During that discussion, one of the principals commented, "This sounds like poorly behaved 8th-graders." This concept of "bullying" became a way for the

A critical friend is "a trusted person who asks provocative questions, provides data to be examined through another lens, and offers critique of a person's work as a friend . . . an advocate for the success of that work [and colleague]."

Costa and Kallick, 1993, p. 50

group to recharacterize and understand Clarke's school and his dilemma. It led the group to reframe Clarke's original question as: What do I need to do about my own leadership practice in order to replace a bullying culture with a more positive culture?

Ellen captured both the high level of empathy that the group held for Clarke and also its commitment to challenge his current response: "There's nothing worse than to sit back and reflect and to be off kilter. And we've all been there. . . . And to know that it's really impacting the way that you want to work in the building and what your priorities are and what you're trying to stress as the most important thing in a building. I'm bringing this forward because . . . it's a very lonely job sometimes and you can isolate yourself, too, when getting out into that crowd, it becomes frightening."

The group went on to suggest ways that Clarke could reframe the dilemma and next steps he might take, including:

- Employing protocols to focus school conversations on teaching and learning
- Establishing clear norms for working together
- Introducing essential questions and establishing shared assumptions to guide faculty meetings
- Implementing strategies to ensure that all voices are heard, not just the negative or loudest ones
- Conducting a faculty survey about school culture to get a clearer and broader understanding
- Redesigning the induction program to ensure that new teachers become part of a more positive culture

Throughout this process, the group worked collaboratively for the sake of one of its members. The group owned and cared about Clarke's problem. Use of the protocol and Sara's facilitation allowed the group to do extended collaborative work for the benefit of a colleague.

The process closed with Clarke's reflection on what he had heard and how it had influenced his thinking. He agreed with the group's assessment that the school had a culture of bullying, and he reflected on the challenge of confronting the adults involved. He also agreed with the group's reframing of the question, and he was able to talk about his feelings about "being off kilter." In his reflection, Clarke's deprivatization of his practice became deeply personal. The process and the collaborative work of the group led him to reflect with colleagues on his challenges as a principal and to craft steps to move forward.

In the final step of the *Consultancy*, Sara asked the group to reflect on the process. The group did not reflect on Clarke's dilemma, but rather on their practice as a group as they enacted the *Consultancy*.

This story illustrates the power of a self-authoring critical friends group in which a member brings a personal issue related to his practice. Clarke trusted his CFG colleagues with a dilemma that was at the heart of what it means to be a leader. Through disciplined use of a protocol guided by an experienced facilitator, the group was able to persistently and thoughtfully uncover and question assumptions underlying the dilemma. With careful listening and focused feedback, the CFG acknowledged the uncertainty and ambiguity of being a leader—a role that is more frequently characterized by control and decisiveness—and offered Clarke a way forward as he took up the challenge of creating a more positive school culture.

A critical friends group, such as the TILE group described here, offers educators an approach to self-authoring learning that can build a school's capacity to transform its practice. It requires a long-term commitment to collaboration that is rigorous in its focus, disciplined in its practice, and persistent in its action.

CLINICAL SUPERVISION:
USING A NONDIRECTIVE APPROACH TO SUPERVISION

As teachers move to engage in self-authoring learning, leaders need to consider how they might adapt their supervisory practices to support teachers. In the collaborative approach to supervision described in relation to socializing learning in Chapter 3, leaders engage in co-creating responses to issues or challenges that teachers are facing. Alternatively, in the nondirective approach, teachers frequently identify their own questions or issues related to their practice. It becomes the role of the leader to assist in framing a response or action. One way a leader might assist a teacher is to help develop an inquiry to examine a question or issue. The leader may even help collect data or analyze the results. Another approach may be to use strategies similar to those of an instructional coach—listening, clarifying, encouraging, and reflecting to help a teacher think through a particular issue or response (Glickman et al., 2010).

A tricky aspect of using a nondirective approach is to determine whether the teacher has the resources (knowledge, experience, and expertise) to create a potentially successful response to a problem or issue. If the issue or problem is outside the teacher's expertise, the leader initially might assist in bringing together the needed resources and then shift to a coaching role.

Leaders also can support teachers who are self-authoring learners by creating opportunities for them to learn and pursue challenging questions in collaboration with others, perhaps through involvement in a CFG, a teacher-led inquiry experience, or a lesson study cycle. As educators move toward self-authoring learning, colleagues develop relationships that foster accountability to and with one another. Educators working with colleagues over time come to entrust aspects of their work that they worry about the most to colleagues, and they come to count on one another to give authentic feedback, challenges to assumptions, and regular follow-up about the progress of their learning. In this way, a leader is not the sole source of support, learning, and even accountability for teacher learning.

SUPPORTING SELF-AUTHORING LEARNING: IMPLICATIONS FOR LEADERSHIP

Instrumental learning asks educators to learn about practices and programs that will improve teaching and learning. Socializing learning asks educators to collaborate with their colleagues to develop shared understanding and agreement about practices of teaching and learning that make a difference for students. Self-authoring learning asks educators to engage in the most challenging and discomforting learning to question the very purpose of schools and the assumptions and oftentimes unexamined beliefs upon which they are based.

Self-authoring learning requires leaders to provide opportunities to raise and dig into challenging questions about assumptions and purposes. However, it is not enough to provide others with these opportunities; leaders of self-authoring learning themselves must be engaged in raising disquieting questions and the resulting dialogue that can transform a school. It is only by being a self-authoring learner can leaders engage others.

Being a Learner as Well as a Leader

Being a leader of self-authoring learning requires being a learner and risk taker. Assuming the role of an active and visible learner demands that leaders operate in ways that are contrary to the frequently held notion that leaders always have the right answers and are decisive in every situation. Leading self-authoring learning requires a leader to take the risks of discussing the undiscussable, asking uncomfortable questions, and engaging in persistent dialogue about purposes and assumptions. Only by seeing the leader as a learner and risk taker will others feel that it is safe to join in the learning.

Posing Challenging Questions

One of the most powerful ways a school leader might support self-authoring learning is to raise questions the school needs to explore. What are the issues that are undiscussable? What are the questions we avoid? Perhaps they are invisible to many in the school, or perhaps they are known but ignored because the school doesn't know how to address them. Leaders might raise these questions themselves, give voice to the educators in the school who are asking them, or work collaboratively with teachers and students to identify the questions the school needs most to ask. If schools are ever to be transformed, the most challenging, anxiety-producing questions need to be asked. Instructional leaders have a particular responsibility to ask these questions at every opportunity. Setting goals, aligning instructional practices, developing curriculum, and looking at data all offer the leader an opportunity to raise questions that lie at the heart of what it means to be a school that pursues transformation of its practice.

Challenges for Leaders

Leaders need to not only engage with school colleagues in the learning, but also prepare and support the school to operate within the ambiguity, anxiety, and unease that invariably result from self-authoring learning. Self-authoring learning that leads to school transformation is not quick or easy. Leaders are challenged to remain steadfast and committed to the long-term transformation of schools in the face of the external and internal pressures to seek easier and quicker solutions. This is risky work. It is particularly risky because leaders are hired to have answers, not questions, and to solve problems, not surface them. The challenge for school leaders is to accept this risk.

Schools experience an incredible push toward action, to find the best solutions and enact them immediately, to address the perceived deficits and shortcomings of students, educators, schools, parents, and society as a whole. However, quick fixes to complex problems are often short-lived and quickly replaced by the newest, best practice. This cycle of adoption, implementation, and abandonment of practices reduces the complex acts of teaching and learning to a series of steps to be implemented or a set of materials to be used. The rush toward the promise of quick fixes belies the complexity of the challenges. As Hargreaves and Shirley (2009) caution, the work of changing schools requires a more thoughtful and disciplined approach. The challenging role of a school leader is to hold and negotiate the tension between the drive toward the immediate response and the need for an adaptive response that requires flexibility and openness (Heifetz et al., 2009).

CHAPTER 5

How Leaders Facilitate for Learning

*The expectation is that we are surfacing and challenging
assumptions, asking probing questions, and bringing real
artifacts—our own work—to the table.*
— *Jennifer Flewelling, Principal,*
North Beverly Elementary School

Instructional leaders typically understand that for schools to improve the
schools, the teams that they work on and even schools themselves need to
learn new teaching approaches, new understandings of how learning happens, and even new ways of working together as professionals. The most
effective instructional leaders not only accept the challenge of this difficult
work but also have a substantial repertoire of strategies, techniques, and
facilitator approaches that increase the likelihood that schools and the adults
who work in them do indeed learn in ways that will benefit their students.

In this chapter we examine some of the most common—and most
useful—strategies and facilitator moves that instructional leaders use to
help educators learn. We discuss not only how to structure the time that
teachers have for meeting, learning, and working together, but also how
to productively facilitate that time. We consider agenda design, norm setting, the use of protocols to support adult learning, and the facilitator
skills that are essential to ensuring that the limited opportunities that
educators have for meeting and learning together result in learning that
helps students. As in other chapters, we begin with an account of adult
learning in a real school.

For Thursday's faculty meeting, Jennifer Flewelling, principal of the
North Beverly Elementary School, asked teachers to bring samples of
student writing from any students about whom they were for some reason or another concerned. Teachers regularly brought artifacts—student
work, lesson plans, interdisciplinary projects, letters to parents—to faculty meetings, so everyone arrived with a few journals, a writing folder,
or a stack of student essays.

Jennifer's agenda indicated that the goals of the meeting were to (1)
build a shared understanding of how different grade levels taught writing,
(2) consider ways teachers could modify their practice to help struggling

students, and (3) think together about the degree to which the school's approach to writing was working for all the school's students. The agenda indicated that the meeting would begin with a whole-group "check-in"—time reserved for the group to exhale, transition from what they had been doing, and prepare for their work together. At the heart of the agenda was a *Collaborative Assessment Conference* (see Appendix A for a description of the protocol) that teachers joined in small groups, followed by a whole-group discussion that Jennifer would facilitate. The agenda also left time at the end for the group to reflect on how the members had worked together.

At the North Beverly Elementary School, Jennifer replaced the typical faculty meeting in which, more often than not, the principal stood in front of the faculty, went down a "to do" list, asked if there were any questions (mostly there weren't), and, with any luck, mercifully let the faculty leave a few minutes early. Jennifer's quite different meeting format combines many structures and practices that support teacher learning: (1) the meeting is an occasion for collegial, collaborative discussions among teachers, (2) the clearly articulated goals of the meeting are focused on improving teaching and learning, (3) teachers are asked to make public their practice by sharing their students' work, (4) a protocol is used to structure the conversation, and (5) teachers are asked to be reflective about how they learned together. Increasing adult learning in schools requires intentionality, persistence, and accomplished leadership.

MEETINGS FOR LEARNING

In general, instructional leaders regard any occasions when teachers are together—faculty meetings, professional development days, grade-level or department meetings—as opportunities for teachers to learn together and to practice the structures and practices that support teacher learning. At the North Beverly faculty meeting, not only did the teachers learn together about the strengths and limits of their writing instruction, but they also practiced following a protocol and reflecting on their group practice.

The literature on facilitation offers two simple but powerful suggestions to instructional leaders who hope to design agendas for meetings that are opportunities for teacher learning (Kaner, Lind, Toldi, Fisk, & Berger, 2007). They are:

1. The agenda should have a clearly articulated learning goal.
2. There should be an equally clear process for reaching that learning goal.

> Any time we are together as a faculty is a time for learning.
> —Jennifer Flewelling, Principal,
> North Beverly Elementary School, Beverly, Massachusetts

The Importance of Clearly Articulated Learning Goals

Because practitioner learning is not always the norm in the schools where many educators work, the instructional leader has to be intentional and persistent about making it happen. This means that the instructional leader, whether she is the principal, team leader, department chair, or teacher leader, needs to articulate an unambiguous learning goal that provides a focus for whatever learning time teachers have.

At the North Beverly Elementary School, whenever the adults meet to work and learn together, they create an agenda that contains the learning goals and a process by which that learning will happen (Figure 5.1 provides such an example). In a faculty meeting the principal often creates the agenda and articulates the learning goal, but teams of teachers, cross-grade-level teams, or departments also can design their own agendas and learning goals. The goals can come from a variety of sources, such as a school improvement plan, a grade-level team's goals, or an ongoing district initiative. A clearly articulated learning goal, no matter who creates it or how it is created, increases the likelihood that adult learning that will make a difference for students actually will happen.

The Importance of a Clear Process for Learning

Meetings that support practitioner learning are clear about process. The North Beverly meetings typically have a structure or protocol that will lead to the particular learning goal the school wants. In the meeting discussed earlier, the faculty used a highly structured and, to them, very familiar process, the *Collaborative Assessment Conference* (which is described in Chapter 3 and can be found in Appendix A), to learn more about the variety of approaches to teaching writing used in the school. Because adult learning is not always intentionally supported in schools, a protocol not only makes the learning more intentional, but also provides the group a means to think about and reflect on their group learning.

Figure 5.1. Agenda for North Beverly Elementary School Meeting—Teacher Version

September 24, 2008

- What do we talk about? How do we talk about it?
- What difference does it make?

Working Hypotheses About Professional Learning Communities

- Schools and school systems that continually challenge themselves to develop professional collaborative learning communities are better able to create conditions that support the learning of schools, leaders, teachers, and especially children.
- There are powerful forces that conspire against schools becoming reflective, collaborative professional communities that can steadfastly focus on issues of teaching and learning.
- Increasingly, schools use structured conversations or protocols to overcome the barriers to professional community and build capacity for reflecting, collaborating, and, most of all, focusing on the work of teaching and learning.

Meeting Goals

1. Continue to build a shared understanding of working hypotheses about professional learning communities

2. Understand the connections between professional learning communities and student learning

3. Draft schoolwide learning goals

Agenda

1. **Connections: What will we learn together?** Introductions, check in, review agenda, working hypotheses

2. **What evidence connects how we talk and what we talk about to student learning?** (Goal 1)
   Text-based discussion: professional learning communities

3. **What are our learning goals? What do we need to learn for the sake of our students?** (Goal 2)
   Small to large group goal-setting

4. Questions/Reflection

The Facilitator's Agenda

A useful tool for any facilitator is a "facilitator's agenda." The facilitator's agenda is a version of the meeting agenda that is just for the facilitator and is full of reminders, critical moves, and important questions. Leading learning is complicated work because facilitators have to make lots of decisions, many of them in the moment, while hoping to get important work done, with a group watching them. Facilitators regularly make decisions, for example, about how the room will be arranged, how the group will be divided, what the speaker order will be, what questions to ask, when to linger over a particular agenda item, and when to push forward.

In a facilitator's agenda, the facilitator adds his or her own reminders and notes; such reminders might include, for example, notes for crucial agenda items, back-up questions, possible room set-up plans, and notes about times for each part of the agenda. The facilitator's agenda is a tool for the facilitator only. The participant agenda is what is shared with the faculty, department, or team. In contrast to the participant agenda shown in Figure 5.1, which was for the teachers, Figure 5.2 shows Jennifer's facilitator agenda from that same meeting.

Facilitating for learning is hard, intricate work, especially with groups that are not comfortable with learning-focused meetings. It makes sense for facilitators to do all the planning that they can.

AGREEMENTS, NORMS, AND GROUND RULES

Why Norms Are So Important

Establishing group agreements is essential to the success of any type of collaborative learning. Group agreements, norms, or ground rules are important because groups always have norms already. For example, groups often have "unspoken rules" or "hidden agreements" about who sits where, whose voice gets heard, or who can leave early or arrive late. These agreements are rarely spoken about, acknowledged, or written down. Further, no one ever asks: Are these the norms that we want? Without an intentional process that asks groups to think about their rules, norms, or agreements, groups will operate—and learn—much as they always have (Argyris, 1999; Schein, 2010; Senge, 2006).

As Joe McDonald and his colleagues (2007) explain, explicit, transparent agreements can both discourage and encourage certain behaviors. For example, the agreement, "honor our time together," can reduce late arrivals and early departures from meetings, whereas, "be curious and listen

Figure 5.2. Agenda for the Facilitator of the North Beverly
    Elementary School Meeting

September 24, 2008

*Facilitator's note: We need to start
promptly at 8:30 and end at 10:30
when the kids come back to their
classrooms.*

*Facilitator's note: We are meeting
in the cafeteria, so we need chart
paper, markers, and stands.*

What do we talk about? How do we talk about it?
What difference does it make?

Working Hypotheses About Professional Learning Communities

- Schools and school systems that continually challenge themselves to develop
  professional collaborative learning communities are better able to create
  conditions that support the learning of schools, leaders, teachers, and
  especially children.
- There are powerful forces that conspire against schools becoming reflective,
  collaborative professional communities that can steadfastly focus on issues of
  teaching and learning.
- Increasingly, schools use structured conversations or protocols to overcome
  the barriers to professional community and build capacity for reflecting,
  collaborating, and, most of all, focusing on the work of teaching and
  learning.

Meeting Goals

1. Continue to build a shared understanding of working hypotheses about
   professional learning communities

2. Understand the connections between professional learning communities and
   student learning

3. Draft schoolwide learning goals

*Facilitator's note: Make sure that
everyone does not sit with their
grade-level team. If they do, have
them count off into small groups.*

Agenda

1. Connections: What will we learn together? (Goal 1)
   Introductions, check in, review agenda, working hypotheses

2. What evidence connects how we talk and what we talk about to student
   learning? (Goal 1)
   Text-based discussion: professional learning communities

> *Facilitator's note: Possible debrief
> questions: What struck you in your
> conversations? What questions
> about how we (NBES) operate does
> this piece raise? What do these
> elements of professional community
> look lie at North Beverly? What
> should they look like?*

> *Facilitator's note: Use the Final Word
> protocol in triads. Try to do this in 20
> minutes and then have a long debrief –
> maybe 15 minutes.*

3. What are our learning goals? What do we need to learn for
   the sake of our students? (Goal 2)
   Small- to large-group learning goal setting

> *Facilitator's note: This should take an hour. Work in triads
> then move to groups of 6 and then 12 before reporting out.
> Each group can only pick three (or four at the most) goals.*

4. Questions/Reflection

*Facilitator's note: Consider asking
them which goal resonated most
with them as a check-out.*

for understanding," can encourage taking on the point of view of others. Norms can help to acknowledge and accommodate different learning styles. "Honor time to think before speaking," can provide the space and time for processing needed by some participants and help others develop empathy for learning needs. And, norms can help us try out new behaviors—"take risks and support others to do so"—and can establish the expectation that the participants will be asked to take on new behaviors in this group. Norms provide a shared understanding of the way we are going to act while we are in a group. They are another structure—like protocols—that helps to create a space of trust, mutual accountability and responsibility, and predictability that is vital for community members to learn from and with one another.

To some, group agreements feel like a waste of time. Typical comments might be, "We are all adults here and know how to work together," or, "We don't need to take time to talk about how we will work," or, "We need to just get started." To others, norms might feel like an unnecessary interference—"Let's just hear from everyone. We all have ideas to add to the conversation." Groups want to keep behaving as they always have, and a discussion about ground rules or norms questions long-standing group behavior. Learning leaders understand that if groups are to learn in new ways, then they need to operate in new ways—or at least make sure that the way they currently operate supports the learning that they need to do.

At Serna Elementary School in San Antonio, Texas, teachers were eager to take up the work of collaboratively reviewing assessment practices and did not see the need to take the time to establish agreements as to how they would work. Jeff Price, the principal, characterized the situation as follows: "The teachers didn't imagine that they needed to prepare for times when they would have differences of opinion or disagreements. Since they had little experience in learning together in a socializing manner, they did not know the demands such learning would make on them." But Jeff did, so he met with each grade-level team and facilitated the development of norms to guide their collaborative work. The results have guided their work ever since (for an example, see Figure 5.3).

Figure 5.3. Sample Norms for Student Work Review

- Participants are nonjudgmental
- Everyone participates
- Everyone looks for questions, patterns, and "I wonder . . . 's"
- Team leaves with a plan of action

How to Establish Norms

There are a number of processes that facilitators use to develop norms with groups (see Appendix D, and Appendix E, for two such examples). The processes vary according to the size of the group, the work it needs to do, and how often the group meets. However, all processes are built on similar thinking:

1. A norm, ground rule, or community agreement is the answer to an essential question such as, "What do I need from the group in order to do my best work or my best learning?" Groups have norms for a purpose.
2. Everyone in the group needs to answer the essential question. Everyone participates. Since the question is about the group, it is important that the answers are also about the group—not about individuals in the group.
3. The answers are shared. Depending on the size of the group, how regularly it meets, and the nature of its work, effective facilitators structure this step in different ways. For example, they limit the number of answers an individual can share, or do a go-around with no repeats. Sometimes facilitators put a time boundary around the sharing by limiting everyone to 30 seconds to share.
4. In large groups, facilitators often have the group work first in pairs and then in fours (and in some cases in eights) to share, prioritize, and synthesize norms.
5. The draft agreements from individuals or groups need to be listed and clarified. Good facilitators always ask whether there is a norm that someone does not quite understand or needs to hear more about.
6. There are two final questions that need to be answered by the whole group. The first is, "Is there any agreement that someone cannot live with?" The second asks, "Is there any agreement that is not on our list that we really need?" These two questions give the group a chance to fine-tune, add, or remove an agreement. If there is a ground rule that not everyone can agree to, it can be amended, dropped from the list, or tried for a specified period of time.

Instructional leaders who skillfully develop norms understand that whatever language the group uses—norms, ground rules, community agreements—these norms can and should be reviewed periodically. Norms are always "draft" norms; agreements are always our "current" agreements; ground rules are always "in progress." Understanding that the norms are always drafts can help a group resist the temptation to wordsmith, over-think, and even use the process to avoid difficult work that the group has to do. Many facilitators end the norm-setting process by saying, "Let's try these out—for a while."

How Norms Continue to Make a Difference

However, it is not enough to craft norms. Because norms are always "in progress," it is important that facilitators have command of multiple strategies that ensure that the norms are serving the group well and the group is adhering to the norms. A simple strategy is to review the norms at the start of each meeting; doing so draws attention to the anticipated way of working together. Starting each meeting with a norms review also begins to establish a shared ritual to mark the shift from the way we used to work together to this new way. A second way is to end the meeting by asking the group to think for a minute about how it enacted the norms. A simple question like, "How did we do today?" can help strengthen the norms and build reflective practice.

To promote its norms as dynamic and useful tools, at the International School of the Americas in San Antonio, the leadership team wrote the faculty's norms on posters that they put up in the common meeting space and created brightly colored laminated copies that could be taken to any meeting at any site around the school. Often, whoever is convening or facilitating the group invites each group member to choose a particular norm that stands out for her, and to share it with the group. Or, each person is invited to privately choose a norm that he wants to pay particular attention to during the session. Another opportunity comes at the end of the meeting, when the group might pause to consider how the norms helped to support the work that it accomplished.

These small but important steps draw attention to the significant shift in behavior that learning in collaborative settings requires. They help mark the move from a "typical" way of being in school to the ways required by collaborative learning—slowing down to learn from the insight, knowledge, and expertise in the group; digging into the complexity of teaching and learning; and reflecting on our practice and the impact it has on our students. And, as the group members learn together, the nature of their work will evolve over time, becoming more complex and nuanced, often requiring that the group's norms change.

UNDERSTANDING THE DESIGN PRINCIPLES: PROTOCOLS FOR LEARNING

The structured conversations or protocols described in Chapter 3 are powerful tools that instructional leaders can use to support practitioner learning in schools. Protocols are useful structures, and they become even more useful when instructional leaders understand the principles upon which they are built.

> The protocol brings everyone to the center in terms of not being the avoiding colleague or the pushy colleague. It makes it safer. The protocol helps us get to our learning goals; it helps us be more rigorous.
> —Julie MacDonald, Assistant Principal,
> Holten Richmond Middle School, Danvers, Massachusetts

The steps of most protocols are designed to go against the grain of interactions that adults usually have in schools. Adults in schools, for the most part, work in isolation, yet every protocol asks them to work with a group of colleagues. In many settings this can be a challenging shift. Besides encouraging collegial work, protocols often support three other "against the grain" interactions. They are: (1) slowing down, (2) sharing practice, and (3) embracing discomfort.

Slowing Down

Slowing down is an "against the grain" practice because educators, for very obvious reasons, are always in a rush. They rush to get their grades done, to pick up their students after recess, to schedule parent conferences, to eat their lunch, to modify lesson plans, and to cover required material. Protocols, on the other hand, ask teachers to slow down. They ask teachers, for example, in the *Collaborative Assessment Conference* (described in Appendix A), not to rush to judgment about student work, but to slow down and really observe it, look carefully at it, and describe it. The *Consultancy* protocol (described in Appendix C) asks teachers to carefully come to grips with a colleague's dilemma of practice by *not* offering suggestions or making judgments until there have been opportunities for clarifying and then probing questions. Text-based protocols ask teachers to deliberately unpack the meaning of a text and build a shared understanding of an important idea rather than to quickly come up with the "correct" answer. Protocols ask groups of teachers to take their time, to exhale, and to slow down in a way that is not typical of their daily practice.

Sharing Practice

Sharing practice is the second "against the grain" interaction that protocols encourage. Teachers talk to one another all the time. They talk about students, they talk about parents, and they talk about the administration. Teachers talk about how much paperwork they have to do, about the new textbook, and about their colleagues. Unfortunately, teachers do not regularly talk about their teaching, and not often in rigorous ways.

My goal is to get the group to start talking about teaching and learning and not about the laminator and not about the transparencies being missing. We need to share our real work and our kids' real work.

—Matt Fusco, Principal,
Great Oak Elementary School, Danvers, Massachusetts

Many protocols encourage teachers to share their practice—to ask for feedback in the *Tuning* protocol (Appendix B) or to present a dilemma in the *Consultancy* (Appendix C). Teacher learning that makes a difference is learning about teaching practice. Well-designed protocols can focus teacher talk on sharing, learning about, and consequently improving their practice.

Embracing Discomfort

Embracing discomfort is the final "against the grain" interaction encouraged by protocols. Schools are often friendly, congenial places, full of sociable, affable adults who have a lot in common. However, significant research suggests that schools are not often collegial, professional places that have the capacity to have challenging conversations about practice (Hargreaves & Shirley, 2009; Lieberman & Miller, 2008; Schmoker, 2006; Wagner, 2004; Wagner & Kegan, 2006). Similarly, research suggests that a school's ability to raise difficult questions, respectfully disagree, and resist easy answers can be a powerful engine that supports teacher learning (Bryk et al., 2010).

The structure of protocols encourages teachers to take risks and live with the discomfort associated with sharing their practice. In the *Collaborative Assessment Conference* (Appendix A), for example, a teacher is asked to take the risk of presenting her students' work, but is not asked to defend the work. She only listens as colleagues first describe and then wonder about the work. In the *Consultancy* (Appendix C), a teacher presents a dilemma of practice but then listens as colleagues discuss the dilemma. Well-designed protocols not only ask presenters to experience the discomfort of presenting a dilemma or student work, but also give them a safe place from which to listen and learn. Eventually, the presenters and their colleagues learn to trust the structure and the learning that they get from it.

At the North Beverly Elementary School, Jennifer explains that the "use of protocols makes it safe for teachers to take the risks needed to push their own and each other's practice." Having a repertoire of structured conversations can be seen as a way of regulating the discomfort of more public and

> If something goes in an uncomfortable direction, I know how to handle the discomfort without ruining the integrity of the process. Eventually we learn to trust the process and each other.
>
> —Jennifer Flewelling, Principal,
> North Beverly Elementary School, Beverly, Massachusetts

more transparent learning as groups move from instrumental to socializing and eventually to self-authoring learning. Protocols can be thought of as a tool for leaders to use to create a "holding environment" that contains just enough safety and risk to transform practice (Heifetz et al., 2009).

FACILITATING PROTOCOLS FOR LEARNING

Protocols are not easy answers, and they certainly don't facilitate themselves. Because the forces that conspire against adult learning in schools are so strong, the effectiveness of protocols in supporting adult learning is directly related to the degree to which protocols are supported by skilled facilitation. McDonald and colleagues (2007) suggest, "At its heart, facilitation is about participation, ensuring equity and building trust" (p. 15).

In many faculty, team, grade-level, or departmental meetings, there is little teacher participation. The principals, team leaders, department heads, and other instructional leaders share information about the upcoming state tests, or talk about a new policy the school board has implemented, or hand out the new schedule; a few teachers ask questions or raise concerns, and then the group moves to the next issue. There is minimal participation and no learning.

Participation is important because, as discussed earlier, teacher learning that improves practice needs to be done collegially and collaboratively. At the North Beverly Elementary School, every teacher participates in every meeting. They all bring student work, use a protocol, and give one another feedback. The facilitator of each group makes sure that everyone shares

> A well-facilitated protocol takes the hierarchy out of the equation. Every voice is heard. All our wisdom is shared.
>
> —Julie MacDonald, Assistant Principal,
> Holten Richmond Middle School, Danvers, Massachusetts

student work, and that they both give and receive feedback about practice. Participation is important because it (1) provides a variety of perspectives that increase the possibility of new insight, and (2) builds a group that is smarter than any individual (McDonald et al., 2007).

However, facilitation that focuses only on participation gets just part of the way toward the adult learning that improves practice. Participation needs to be coupled with equity. When skilled facilitators talk about "hearing all voices," they acknowledge both that some voices often are not heard, and that important learning is lost when that happens. The missing voices are often the voices that not only have a perspective that challenges a group's assumptions, but also can create the dissonance that can result in important learning. Facilitation that focuses on equity of voice ensures that the group does not keep having the conversation that it has always had.

Skilled facilitation also builds trust. However, this does not mean that everyone on the North Beverly faculty has to trust everyone else or that everyone is always comfortable in these new conversations. It does not mean that everyone in the small groups that looked at student work together trusts everyone else. Facilitation that builds trust does so by building trust in the process. The North Beverly faculty trusts that the processes that they use will help them learn, help them improve their writing program, and help the students who struggle the most. For teachers to learn about their practice, especially about the elements of their practice that they struggle with, they need to trust enough to share their practice and trust that the process will result in learning that they could never access without the group. Facilitation that builds trust protects both the presenter and the integrity of the process.

Facilitator Moves

Good facilitation makes a difference. In our experience, there are key facilitator "moves" that influence how teams, departments, and faculties learn. We offer ten moves that we find particularly useful when facilitating adult learning.

Facilitator Move 1: Openings are important. The literature on group practice suggests that how a meeting begins can have a major impact on how it turns out (Kaner et al., 2007). At the North Beverly Elementary School, meetings begin with a "check-in" that provides an opportunity for teachers to say whatever they need in order to refocus themselves for the work they are about to do. In these few minutes some teachers talk about a student they are concerned about, others thank someone for covering their class the previous day, a few talk about their stress around an upcoming report card night, some write in their journals, and others sit quietly. Other versions of check-in are *Open Circle* (*Open Circle*, n.d.) and *Connections*

(Thompson-Grove, n.d.). Good facilitative practice suggests that beginnings, whether a whole-group check-in, introductions in new groups, or a review of agendas and the group's norms, are important facilitator moves that increase the likelihood of a productive meeting full of adult learning.

Facilitator Move 2: Closings are also important. The way a meeting ends also impacts learning. The final step of each meeting should be to engage in some type of feedback or group debrief. For example, at North Beverly Elementary School, there is always a group debrief. The principal always asks for feedback—written or spoken—about the meeting. Similarly, the final step of every well-designed protocol asks the group to reflect on its enactment of the protocol.

This facilitator move recognizes that groups improve their own practice only when they intentionally reflect on and learn about their group practice; that is, when they intentionally work to learn about how they learn (Argyris, 1999). This type of reflection is not common in schools, and it takes a skilled and committed facilitator to ensure that it happens.

Facilitator Move 3: Understand why you are using a particular protocol. Engaging in "against the grain" practices that encourage teacher learning does not always make adults comfortable. It can be uncharted, uncomfortable territory. Facilitators frequently hear comments such as, "Can't we just skip this touchy-feely stuff?" or, "Why do we need a structure; can't we just talk like we always do?" or, "I don't really care what happens in the other grades," or, "What are we really accomplishing here?" Not only are comments such as these common, they are to be expected. The challenge is not to find a way to avoid them, but to put them in the proper context and learn from them.

Protocols are designed with a particular learning goal in mind. The *Collaborative Assessment Conference* helps build a shared understanding of issues of teaching and learning, while helping an individual teacher gain new insight about a particular student or group of students. The *Tuning* protocol

> The "closure" of our meetings is more framed. It is a time to reflect. Sometimes we use a prompt, "Now I think . . . " or, "What I learned was . . . " Sometimes we ask a question like, "How did we do?" We always take time to reflect.
>
> —Jennifer Flewelling, Principal,
> North Beverly Elementary School, Beverly, Massachusetts

is designed to produce useful feedback about a product such as a lesson plan or unit design, and can raise issues of curriculum coherence. In the *Consultancy*, an educator asks colleagues for help in better understanding a dilemma of professional practice. The *Final Word* protocol is an effective way for a group to learn together about a complex idea, strategy, or practice contained in a text. Each protocol is designed for a specific purpose, and it is the facilitator's responsibility to make sure that the protocol's design lines up with the group's learning goals and the presenting educator's question (McDonald et al., 2007). A mismatched protocol sometimes can be more harmful than no protocol at all.

Facilitator Move 4: Plan the protocol. As with any learning experience, planning can increase the odds that learning actually will happen. Good facilitators regularly pre-conference with the teacher bringing student work or presenting a dilemma of practice before the group gets together. The purpose of this conversation is to make sure (1) that the facilitator understands exactly what type of feedback the presenter wants, and (2) that the process that the group will use is suited for producing the feedback that the presenter needs. It is not helpful for teachers to take the risk of bringing a dilemma of practice or student work to a group and not get the feedback that they need, or of participating in a process with which they are uncomfortable.

Facilitator Move 5: Explain the protocol. Experienced facilitators understand that groups can easily stray from a protocol and wander back into their usual and more comfortable ways of talking and working together. From the very beginning, groups need to be reminded about the purpose of the protocol and what the steps are. Effective facilitation always answers the questions, "Why are we doing this?" and, "How is this going to work?" This explanation or review of the protocol also could provide an opportunity to connect group norms to the work the protocol requires or asks of the group.

Facilitator Move 6: Facilitate the entire protocol. Because the pull of our typical group practice is so strong, groups can easily lose track of where they are in a particular structure. Comments such as, "Can't we just leave out this step?" or, "Let's just solve the problem!" or, "Why do we have to spend so much time on description?" often are heard. Skilled facilitators continually remind the group of where they are in the process, and they ensure that everyone has a chance to participate before the group moves ahead. If, for example, in a *Consultancy*, some members of the group want to shorten the step of clarifying questions, the group runs the risk of losing the voices, knowledge, and wisdom of those members who still need to understand the dilemma. The facilitator should pay attention to time, stick to the protocol, and use the debriefing step at the end to figure out how it went.

Facilitator Move 7: Don't be afraid to facilitate. Skilled facilitators often remind a group that facilitation is important to achieving the group's learning goals. Typical reminders include, "I am going to do a little facilitating now," or, "It might make sense if I do a little more facilitating," or, "If it is all right with the group, I am going to take a more facilitative role right now." When the conversation starts to move too fast, if voices are left out or the discussion gets uncomfortable, these reminders help the group refocus and ensure that the conversation stays productive. They also let the group know that the facilitator is taking responsibility for the group's learning. Sometimes, when the facilitator knows in advance that the conversation might be complicated or anxiety-producing, she might announce that she will facilitate the protocol very closely, in order to let the group know that someone is working hard to ensure that their time together is as productive as possible. Other times the facilitator might even review the norms the group has agreed upon. The point is that the facilitator must facilitate.

Facilitator Move 8: Never forget to debrief the process. Because schools are not always reflective places, the question, "How did we do?" is infrequently asked. Yet, if schools are ever to become more reflective, they need to think about the processes they use. Questions like, "How did we do?" "What did we learn about process?" "Did the processes help us get what we want?" and "What will help us work together better the next time?" can be used to prompt reflection. However, it is the facilitator's responsibility to ensure that the reflection that improves learning processes regularly takes place. Don't skip this last step—build it into the process.

Facilitator Move 9: Find a place for negative questions and comments. Good facilitation also ensures that there is a proper place for negative questions and comments. Comments such as, "Why can't we talk like we usually do?" or, "What are we really accomplishing here?" belong in the reflection part of the meeting or protocol. These questions and comments are important to hear and can inform the design of the next learning experience, but if there is no space for reflection about the process, these questions surface elsewhere and can be seen as inappropriate and distracting. A good facilitator acknowledges the importance of these comments and reassures the person who makes them that there will be a place for the group to consider them.

The Most Important Facilitator Move

Facilitator Move 10: Trust the process and trust the group. When Jennifer talks about her efforts to lead learning at North Beverly Elementary School, she freely admits that "trusting the process and the group have been my greatest challenge and most powerful learning." It is often very difficult for leaders to resist an easy answer, to sit with open questions, and to tolerate ambiguity; after all, it often seems like providing answers is their job (Heifetz & Linsky, 2002). Yet to the degree that leaders provide answers, they also limit the capacity of the school to learn. Jennifer argues, "If I cannot admit to the school that I am uncomfortable or anxious and have things to learn, then how can I expect them to take risks and be learners?" Supporting adult learning in schools means the leader needs to trust the process and the group, and be a learner herself.

CHAPTER 6

How Leaders Design for Learning

As the previous chapters have described, there are structures and strategies that can be used to help a school to initiate, deepen, and transform the learning of adults in the school, and there are facilitation practices that can be used to enact those learning experiences in ways that support teacher learning. In this chapter we help leaders think about how to design and implement plans for school learning. We consider how instructional leaders might decide among strategies and structures to use and why they might make those choices.

The chapter is organized around three levels of learning leaders have to manage as they design and lead for adult learning in their schools: school learning, teacher learning, and leader learning. In any school or group, instructional leaders have the complex task of designing learning that supports learning at every level. Because leading for learning and focusing on each of these levels is complex work, there are no easy how-to's or lists. This is also, of course, because each context is unique. Therefore, our approach is to provide a framework of design questions targeted at each of the three levels: school, teacher, and leader.

Leaders have to make decisions, anticipate trade-offs and losses, and tolerate the ambiguity and complexity that accompany trial and error. This chapter provides a framework to assist in the diagnosis and decision-making process, and it also anticipates possible challenges based on the advice of our colleagues, school leaders who have navigated this complex territory. Heifetz and colleagues (2009) emphasize the importance of diagnosis, calling it "the single-most important skill and most undervalued capacity" (p. 7). We recommend that instructional leaders take the time for diagnosis and design before implementing any of the structures or strategies described in the book. By considering the tensions and essential questions regarding school, teacher, and leader learning, leaders have a better chance of designing and leading adult learning that will make a difference for the students in their schools. These questions include:

1. What does our school (and its students) need us to learn?
2. Who are our teachers?
3. Who am I as a learner and leader?

DESIGN QUESTION 1: WHAT DOES OUR SCHOOL (AND ITS STUDENTS) NEED US TO LEARN?

The first design question focuses on the school and looks at what the educators in the school might need to learn on behalf of students and their learning. Because looking at what a school needs to learn might feel familiar to leaders, we want to emphasize that this first question has more to do with school learning than school improvement. We propose that instructional leaders seeking to use an adult-learning framework ask questions such as, What adult learning would benefit the students with whom we work? or, What learning must the adults in our school do on our students' behalf?

The emphasis of this book is on the processes of school learning— "how" schools learn. We know that the content of a school's learning— "what" schools need to learn—is unique to each school and context. In this section we propose two ways to consider what the school might learn that connect to using structures described in the previous chapters: taking stock of existing learning initiatives and looking at the school's curriculum. Once diagnostic thought has gone into "what" the school needs to learn, the design of "how" that learning can happen comes into play.

Taking Stock of Existing Learning Initiatives

One way to start the work of figuring out what a school needs to learn is to look at what is currently in place in terms of school learning initiatives. Taking stock of what learning initiatives are happening currently, the nature of those initiatives (instrumental, socializing, self-authoring), who is involved, and what outcomes are being achieved, can be a good starting place for design and diagnosis. It also can illuminate areas where school learning of a particular content or type has not been happening.

Design Check: What are we already learning and how are we learning it? By taking stock, leaders can prevent adding one more initiative to the mix without figuring out how it fits into the bigger picture of school learning. They can avoid multiple initiatives aimed at a similar goal, or even multiple efforts that do not work well together. It also helps leaders to take stock of capacity for school learning and where support for instrumental, socializing, or self-authoring learning might be needed.

During his first year as principal of Serna Elementary in San Antonio, Jeff Price realized, "I was assuming socializing learning at my school. I thought we were a lot further along in terms of collaboration. I assumed that teachers were sharing with each other, for example, on grade-level teams." When he realized the school needed support to move toward more socializing learning, Jeff and his leadership team began to put in place additional scaffolding structures and practices to support the socializing learning initiatives he had already implemented. In his second and third years, Jeff and his school worked carefully and consistently with the socializing structures and practices, as described in Chapters 3 and 5, including setting norms for grade-level teams' work with one another. "Now we are moving . . . from compliance to holding each other accountable. We ask ourselves— why aren't we going to scale on this? Why aren't we seeing school learning? When we're not, we know it's often because teachers aren't sharing their work and learning, especially learning from our successes. We can't go to scale without sharing our work."

Design Check: Are we listening to others? It is important to include others in the process of taking stock. This is a good time to engage not only with a school's leadership team but also with teachers, families, and especially students to consider what the school might need to learn. Each of these constituencies experiences school in a different way, and inquiring as to student, family, and teacher perceptions develops not only important data but also pathways for communication and dialogue.

And, while leaders provide leadership for school learning, they are not the only ones who can participate in or lead this diagnostic process—indeed, if they are the only ones asking the questions and coming up with the answers, they likely will be missing important insights, ideas, data, and voices—and they may end up seeing what they already think or perceive. Some questions that might spark a shared inquiry include the following:

- What do students most need us to learn? How do we know?
- What are strengths of students' current learning and school experiences?
- What are challenges?
- How would student learning be better if teacher practice were to change?

Kathleen Cushman (2003, 2010) and the What Kids Can Do organization (What Kids Can Do, 2011) have developed several interview questionnaires, strategies, and reports, especially ones that feature students as the inquirers into their own learning and what supports it. As Cushman reminds us, students are in the best position to tell us what students think, how they are experiencing classrooms and the school, and where they see strengths as well as areas for improvement.

> We decided to ask the students to describe the teacher they liked the best, and also the teacher from whom they learned the most. Were those two different, and if so, why and how?
>
> Cushman, 2003, p. 185

In her research for *Fires in the Bathroom: Advice for Teachers from High School Students* Cushman asked students, "So what would you suggest to a teacher?" She found that students' suggestions often came from examples of effective teachers, meaning that they wanted other teachers to emulate aspects of the effective teachers' teaching practice, ability to foster classroom community, and willingness to engage in meaningful learning relationships with students. To develop questions to ask students, she also asked several groups of teachers: "What would you ask your students if you could ask them anything about what or how you teach?" To those who want to make school better she recommends: "Taking seriously students' evaluations of their teachers could help identify the masters among a faculty, and allow them to share their approaches with their colleagues" (2003, p. 188).

Examining the School's Curriculum

One specific place for schools to take a careful look is in the area of curriculum. Curricular analysis is important for school learning because it deals with student learning, teacher practice, and school outcomes. What are teachers teaching, how are they teaching, and what are the student learning outcomes? Working together to develop better or more cohesive curriculum on behalf of students and their learning can be a promising and productive focus for adult learning.

Jennifer Flewelling, principal of the North Beverly Elementary School, worked with her school to develop learning goals focused on curriculum, including its cohesiveness: "Some of the areas that we need work on are math instruction and really plugging holes in district-approved curriculum. We want to look at how to best use time. We are asking ourselves—if what we are doing isn't working, can we do something more cohesive?"

Looking at what a school is teaching helps to get below the surface, especially below the surface of test scores, and can lead to important connections to school and teacher practices. Glickman and colleagues (2010) remind us that "curriculum, when treated as a task for school action, is a powerful, relatively non-threatening intervention for enhancing collective thought and action about instruction" (p. 379). The approaches and strategies described in this book lend themselves well to looking at what schools are teaching and how they are teaching in order to move student and school learning forward.

Design Check: How deep are we digging? Curricular examination that goes below the surface, usually of outcomes or effects like test scores, can help to point out larger patterns or root causes. Justin Vernon, principal of the Roger Clap Innovation School in the Boston public schools, describes how he started to think about his school's learning when he came on board as a new principal.

> There were several factors I considered. I started with my initial data analysis, including the state English language arts and science tests. One statistic that really stood out to me and that I started talking with my staff about was that one-fourth of the open-response science questions resulted in a score of zero for our students. That really got to me and I started thinking about how to address that, especially regarding students' writing. Then I did entry interviews with all of the teachers. I had a list of several questions, and one of the questions was, "What do we need to focus on in terms of instruction at our school?" The idea of writing came up several times. From there, I put forward several things we were going to focus on: writing, parent involvement, and really collaborating. But that idea of writing was front and center.

Like Justin, many leaders take stock using test data—and they know that test data tell only part of the story of the school's learning needs. Justin also talked with teachers and did his own analysis about priorities and first steps. This kind of curricular focus centered Justin, and the teachers, on what the school needed to learn so that student learning would benefit.

The learning-focused initiatives described in this book are ones that will support going deeper—and as such it not only takes time to design them but also requires that they be engaged in over time. Significant and substantive curricular examination, as well as efforts to take stock and address school learning, will take time and sustained effort.

DESIGN QUESTION 2: WHO ARE OUR TEACHERS?

The learning of students and the school depends on the learning of teachers. So, while focusing on teacher learning in this design question, of course, relates to school learning (Question 1), in this area instructional leaders have to address the complexity of how to support the learning of individual teachers within collective initiatives and structures. This means considering questions such as: Who are our teachers as learners? How do they learn and what are the implications for leading their learning? How does a leader know where to start in terms of focusing the school's learning efforts, knowing that not everyone needs the same thing? And, what other factors in addition to adult learning should a leader take into account?

Knowing Teachers Well

First, as leaders know, each school, district, department, or grade-level team consists of a unique constellation of teachers. The challenge here is getting to know individual teachers, while also planning for groups of teachers, while also keeping an eye to the school's needs, and throughout that, figuring out what role the leader should play. Not to mention that the dynamics of any group are always distinctive and of course always changing. As one principal put it, "Working with teachers is all about building relationships." Working to get to know teachers as individuals and a part of a group is important if learning is going to be meaningful.

Just as teachers plan with their specific students' faces and needs in mind, Kathy Bieser, principal of the International School of the Americas, describes checking in with a few different teachers as she and her leadership team are planning faculty learning experiences so she can anticipate how different types of learners will respond to the plan. From there, she takes their feedback and insights and builds in additional support or autonomy for instrumental, socializing, and self-authoring learners. This consultation also prevents the leadership team from working in ways in which they themselves feel comfortable, as she knows that might not always work to the faculty's benefit.

Another thing Kathy has learned along the way is that how she frames and introduces a meeting or professional learning experience is important. Now she communicates not only the goals and processes of the meeting but also how she anticipates that each part of the agenda will work for different learners and their needs. By knowing her teachers well, she can help teachers to anticipate what may feel challenging and therefore frustrating, or even too "easy" or "boring" and therefore frustrating. This helps her facilitation during learning meetings as well.

> I've become much more transparent in what we are doing and why. For example, I know the self-authoring teachers need to know "why"—and when I tell them why we are doing something, people rise to their best. I've also learned I have to put my game face on—I have to be confident and open—I don't apologize for things different learners won't like—because I have to be confident and know our plan

is going to be good for teachers, teacher learning, and our school. I can't apologize for it. But I do have to take responsibility for it. That means I have to be open to what is going to happen and adjust, adapt, keep working at it with the teachers, the leadership team, and myself.

Kathy's insights bring to life Heifetz and colleagues' (2009) description of the leader's job: "to mobilize and sustain people through the period of risk that often comes with adaptive change, rather than trying to convince them of the rightness of your causes" (p. 18).

Design Check: Is the group instrumental, socializing, or self-authoring? When a particular structure or strategy described in this book is oriented to a particular type of learner—instrumental, socializing, or self-authoring—its use gives learners ways to participate in learning that both support and challenge them. Yet there will be times when teachers have to work within a structure that challenges their learning—for example, instrumental learners participating in socializing structures. Again the tension is to find ways to both support and challenge—creating "holding environments" for individual teachers and groups—knowing that school learning requires planning with the school and big picture in mind (Heifetz et al., 2009). It is the leader's job to create a holding environment that helps groups develop a capacity for more challenging learning, so that instrumental learning can become socializing learning, and socializing learning can move toward self-authoring learning.

Some of the structures described in this book can be made more (or less) complex in terms of their learning demands for different learners. For example, leaders can select from a study group (instrumental), a learning community (socializing), and a critical friends group (self-authoring) when thinking about groups of teachers learning together. Sometimes leaders might make all options available to teachers for selection—with all of the planning and follow-up that each requires. Some schools allow choice from among several socializing structures, for example, so that collectively the school is working together to share practice and build socializing learning.

Leaders have to choose a starting point with a structure (or structures) that they know will address the needs of the school as well as the predominant needs of the group. From there they will work to build in additional supports like norms and facilitation, and they will have to think in advance about how to anticipate the responses of teachers who will feel vulnerable and want more support. At some point, leaders have to pick a direction, knowing that they are working for the greatest good of the organization, group, or school. Leaders also should know that starting structures are simply where the school starts, not where it will remain. Instrumental and socializing structures and experiences help to build knowledge, skills, and dispositions for self-authoring learning experiences.

Diversity and Teacher Learning

In addition to adult learning and developmental diversity, we want to propose that leaders take other forms of diversity into account when they design for school learning. Race, ethnicity, culture, language, class, age, geography, religion, political opinion, sexuality, values, traditions, ideology, styles of communication, expressions of emotion, life and educational experience, personalities, and more all contribute to individual difference (Achinstein, 2002; Achinstein & Aguirre, 2008; Drago-Severson, 2009; Singleton & Linton, 2006). They also influence teachers' interactions, communication, and collaboration with one another, school leaders, students, and the community.

Two of these differences are particularly salient when designing for adult learning in schools—age and race. These two factors can affect teachers' willingness to learn and collaborate together because they relate to perceptions of power and inclusiveness, school culture and dynamics, and feelings of trust. Challenging notions of seniority, for example, or asking difficult questions about equity, is likely to create discomfort and disequilibrium that leaders should anticipate as they design for school learning.

Design Check: How much do we know about Generation Y teachers? As Chapter 2 discusses, the "greening" of the teaching population is a demographic trend to keep in mind when designing teacher learning. In fact, the most common experience level for teachers in the profession right now is 1 year, which means a large number of "Gen Y" teachers are in our schools now (Ingersoll & Merrill, 2010). Instructional leaders and teachers may already have noticed some generational commonalities among these younger teachers. For example, they are usually comfortable using high-functioning technology (and multitasking with that technology during meetings and other events). These teachers also have experienced a great deal of education (including early childhood education and both school and non-school-related activities), and many have chosen to join the profession because they see it as a way to contribute to social change and act on their moral values (Behrstock-Sherrat & Coggshall, 2010). Gen Y teachers are used to, and therefore often looking for, frequent feedback and affirmation.

When designing and supporting teacher learning, it can help leaders to know that most Gen Y teachers expect to work with supportive school administrators and leaders (including instructional leaders such as grade-level leaders, department chairs, team leaders, and others), and their expectation of "support" includes getting regular and in-depth feedback as well as affirmation. They also expect to be welcomed by their colleagues and be given assistance and support. This may or may not be similar to teachers with different generational experiences and expectations.

So, for example, while novice teachers tend to have instrumental learning needs in terms of learning new curricular content and school procedures, they often are also socializing learners looking for and expecting socializing learning experiences in the company of novice and multigenerational colleagues. Therefore, mentoring programs and support for novice teachers in Gen Y might include instrumental, socializing, and self-authoring features.

Approaches for working with Gen Y teachers align with many of the structures described in Chapters 2, 3, and 4, for example, instructional coaching, peer observation, and learning communities (for these approaches see Figure 6.1). These recommendations also can help leaders to frame their clinical supervision work with Gen Y teachers, especially to know that Gen Y teachers have come to expect frequent feedback.

Design Check: What do veteran teachers need to learn? How do they influence school learning? There are cultural dynamics to anticipate with this influx of new teachers who are part of Gen Y. As described, they have specific generational experiences with schooling, as well as certain expectations regarding their professional work. Yet school cultures tend to reinforce privatized practice, isolation, and seniority (Johnson & Donaldson, 2007). These factors can cause a potent mix when new teachers interact with more experienced colleagues who often expect cultural norms of seniority and isolation to persist. For example, more experienced teachers or older teachers

Figure 6.1. Approaches for Working with Generation Y Teachers

Researchers Behrstock-Sherrat and Coggshall (2010, pp. 33–34) provide specific approaches that can help leaders to "maximize the promise" of these newest and youngest teachers.

- Provide opportunities for Generation Y teachers to receive regular feedback from knowledgeable administrators as well as from peers
- Use student work samples and student achievement data to make this feedback concrete and credible
- Have others observe a Generation Y teacher who has mastered an instructional practice
- Provide opportunities for significant intergenerational learning . . . build true professional learning communities in which young teachers share their collaborative skills, knowledge of social media, and the research-based instructional strategies learned in preparation programs with veteran teachers who, in turn, share their experience-based knowledge of content and how children learn

might resent the voice, participation, and even leadership of younger or less experienced teachers who are perceived to be challenging more traditional perceptions of seniority and privatized practice. In contrast, many novice teachers expect to participate as equal and invested members of the school community and, based on their interest in social change, want to get involved to "make changes" in schools and the system. Instructional leaders have to be ready to anticipate and respond to these tensions.

Using socializing structures, particularly those that involve norms, protocols, and facilitation, can help to "level the field" for teachers and school learning. As Jennifer says: "It's important to take the hierarchy of status out of the equation and level the playing field. The hierarchy must be shattered, so that the third-year teacher becomes equally important as the most experienced. It definitely makes it safer for a new person to jump in. It becomes an expectation that she is part of the conversation and that she will jump in. It can also keep people on track so that some people are not just sharing war stories."

Learning that takes advantage of multigenerational knowledge and expertise benefits schools. Aiming for that and keeping generational dynamics in mind when designing can help leaders be proactive, as otherwise groups might resent a leader's inability to anticipate and alleviate these dynamics.

Design Check: What difference does race make in a school's learning? Another dynamic for leaders to consider when designing school learning with teachers in mind is the diversity of the school in terms of race. What is the racial, ethnic, linguistic, and cultural diversity of the teachers in the school? What is the school's capacity for interracial dialogue?

In her foreword to Singleton and Linton's *Courageous Conversations About Race*, Gloria Ladson-Billings (2006) writes: "Race is the proverbial 'elephant in the parlor.' We know it's right there, staring us in the face—making life uncomfortable and making it difficult for us to accomplish everything we would like to do—but we keep pretending it isn't" (p. x). Because race affects school culture and how teachers work together, and because it is a factor that affects student achievement, three specific design considerations can support interracial dialogue and learning: (1) grouping, (2) use of time, and (3) attention to language (Singleton & Linton, 2006). While these strategies are intended specifically for courageous conversations about race, we think these strategies can help leaders design school learning for teachers in the school as well.

First, when bringing teachers together for professional learning, leaders should pay attention to how they group the teachers. Heterogeneous groups can create a better chance of hearing multiple racial points of view (within and across races), and this can help to prevent the domination of a particular cultural communication style (Singleton & Linton, 2006). Groups optimally consist of an even distribution of White teachers and teachers of color, and heterogeneous groups also should commingle academic departments, grade levels, and other patterns. Leaders also might consider using groups larger than four to provide for more perspectives and interpretations.

Leaders also should pay attention to time in their design. This means making sure there is enough time in activities that call for dialogue so that all participants can share their feelings, feel listened to, and thereby feel validated (Singleton & Linton, 2006). It also means holding to established time parameters and watching, or helping groups to watch, how the group and individuals are using the time allotted for talking. Protocols and norms can help bring attention to time and equitable distribution of talk, although if facilitators are more focused on time than on equitable participation, they can cut off conversation to adhere to time limits.

Finally, in teacher learning experiences, especially those that are designed specifically for dialogue about race and equity, leaders can improve chances of going deeper and having more significant conversations if they spend time in their design process really thinking about the language they use and that teachers will use. For example, for conversations about race, Singleton and Linton (2006) recommend using prompts that are clearly worded and racially focused in order to prevent avoidance and confusion.

Race is a part of the experience of teachers in schools, and it is a part of students' experiences and achievement. Designs for school learning that think about how to promote better interracial dialogue when teachers come together can help to promote teachers' discussion about their practice, the school's practice, and implications for student learning. This short discussion only highlights race as an important and complex dynamic that affects teacher learning. Other chapters in this book include more resources for leaders regarding equity-based conversations, and we recommend the work of Singleton and Linton (2006), Pollock (2008), and others.

DESIGN QUESTION 3: WHO AM I AS A LEARNER AND LEADER?

It All Starts with the Leader

Leaders might start their design considerations where we did, by focusing on the first and second essential questions, which deal with the school and teachers, rather than on themselves. That does not mean this question is the least essential—it is as important as the first two, if not more so. We believe that leading for learning depends on the leader and requires leadership. Leaders not only have to design with school and teacher learning in mind—they also have to consider their role as designers and leaders. This requires looking at who they are as learners, and stopping to consider the relationship between learning and leading. Leaders might ask: Who am I as a learner? Who am I as a leader of learning? What is the relationship between how I learn and how I lead? Leaders who can think about themselves as learners and identify implications for their leadership have made an important link between their leadership and the student, teacher, and organizational learning that improves schools (Drago-Severson, 2009).

Who Am I as a Learner?

The first part of this book described ways of knowing: instrumental, socializing, and self-authoring. We hope instructional leaders saw themselves in these chapters, as both learners as well as leaders responsible for others' learning. It is important that leaders take the time to identify each of these carefully—and separately. Leaders have to know how they learn. They also should know what their tendency is when it comes to leading learning for teachers.

Kathy knows she tends to be a self-authoring learner. For example, in her district's principals' meetings, she is often among those asking questions about the purposes of policies and programs, while others might be asking implementation questions. In her role as the principal and designer of learning for others at the International School, she likes to work in that realm as well—and it fits well with her leadership responsibilities as the instructional leader of a small, progressive magnet school. Because teachers at this small school are the only teacher per course and grade level in their content, and because the school adheres to not only the state standards but also the tenets of the Asia Society International Studies Schools Network (2011) and the advanced placement coursework demands of the College Board (2011), there are complex self-authoring demands for the school's and teachers' practice in terms of curriculum development, integration, and coherence.

Kathy uses her self-authoring insights to develop school learning plans. She also has learned that while it is the school's work and the way she works, not all teachers are comfortable with the high degree of self-authoring learning activity at the school. She knows that socializing learning supports teachers in working for 4-year coherence within the disciplines, and it also helps to support other school goals such as the development of the 4-year portfolio. Therefore, with her teachers and school goals in mind, she plans for socializing learning, and she has learned that she has to keep checking herself to make sure she does not make the socializing learning initiatives more self-authoring based on her own inclinations.

Additionally, she has learned in her 4 years as principal, and after many initiatives and "experiments," to better anticipate the possible responses of teachers who are different learners and to build in stronger scaffolding and support structures. Kathy says:

My goal is to move my school and teachers further toward the edge of self-authoring learning. While I'm comfortable in that realm, I also know that engaging solely in that kind of activity, self-authoring or even socializing learning, can cause some people great frustration, which can turn into shutting down or feeling insecure. Then they can't really participate well. I try to plan for that and keep my teachers in mind when I plan for our faculty learning experiences.

Design Check: Can an instrumental learner lead socializing or self-authoring learning? It might be natural for leaders to envision leading in the way they learn. They have an understanding of the participants' expectations and needs and can design and communicate that. Where it might get tricky for some leaders is to envision leading learning in ways they themselves do not learn. We ended each chapter regarding instrumental, socializing, and self-authoring learning with recommendations for the leader, and in the next section we discuss leading for learning as experimental—leaders learn by and from leading. Still, there are times when instructional leaders may not be the ones best situated to design or lead some initiatives. Instructional leaders have to think carefully about who they are as learners and what that means for embracing new leadership challenges by either leading a new initiative or finding the right leader(s) for that learning. For example, instrumental learning initiatives requires some kind of expertise—if the leader does not have it, then she has to either develop it or find someone who has it. This requires honesty, humility, and a willingness to share leadership for learning.

Sharing leadership does not mean abdicating responsibility or disengaging—in order to be successful, all learning initiatives in the school need the leader's support (in multiple forms, including dedication of time and resources), learning, modeling, and often (depending on the initiative and the leader) participation. These are significant opportunities to learn. Additionally, the leader, as someone who is focused on the school's learning and who knows the teachers well, is in a great position to help design the learning. Thus, leaders might help to design and yet not be the ones to implement. This kind of participation makes sure the learning is tailored to the context and its needs, and it keeps the initiative coherent in the school's learning plan.

Sharing leadership has the benefit of engaging others, especially teachers, in the school's learning. As Jennifer says, "There is usually so much more credibility when teachers get up and teach than when I do, and also much more energy and better group dynamics. They happen to be the experts. My job is not to be the expert on everything—I have to be focused on adult learning." Socializing and self-authoring teachers in particular are eager to contribute to school learning (e.g., leading critical friends groups or convening learning communities), and all teachers have expertise to share with their colleagues (an inviting way to engage instrumental learners).

Design Check: Am I leading with an experimental mind-set? In reflecting on some of first leadership moves in his first year as principal, Justin reflected: "I think had some good leadership moments. And there are many that you make that aren't good. I walked away grateful for the good ones. You hit the sweet spot on the bat occasionally. I still don't know what made me think of it all, but I do think I was thinking with a leadership lens, constantly thinking about how this is going to come off and how the teachers will respond."

Heifetz and colleagues (2009), and others, would agree with Justin's assessment in that not all of the hits will find the sweet spot. In fact, learning leaders learn from all "at bat" attempts, especially if they adopt an "experimental mindset" (p. 15). Jennifer notes, "Learning how *not* to do something is just as valuable. I think that is what makes our process different. We consistently cycle back—we keep talking about it, cycling back, and following up."

Self-authoring learner/leaders might embrace the experimental mind-set in terms of design and assessment. Socializing learner/leaders might work with others as they design and experiment, in which case they should not forget their own insights and instincts. Instrumental learner/leaders might find this experimental mind-set challenging. Jennifer describes her own evolution as a learner and leader: "I started as an instrumental learner—my script was rigid. Now I am far more adaptable and flexible. I know how to intervene and guide the conversation. I know what to do now and feel more comfortable in my abilities. I also have a bag of tricks—including when to insert humor, to be very transparent, and to acknowledge when you are uncomfortable. I now know that it's OK when we are uncomfortable; no one is going to suffocate." This confidence that "no one is going to suffocate" also helps Jennifer to trust the process and let it run its course rather than stopping it when things get uncomfortable for different learners (as they will).

Jennifer learned to broaden her leadership approaches, adapt her leadership, and build her repertoire because she believes that "to get to the next level, a leader must be a learner and a risk taker. I am not the expert and it is not hard for me to say that. My job is to say, Here is the problem and what are we going to do?"

Design Check: The things some people like . . . Once a leader understands how she learns, and how she is acting as a leader, then she can start to figure out how that is going to interact with the needs and expectations of others. A department chair might realize, reflecting on her work with one of her colleagues: "No wonder Tom keeps asking for a lesson plan template from me and ignores every deadline I give him for turning in lesson plans—he's an instrumental learner who needs a clear structure and expectations and I'm a self-authoring learner who believes in giving everyone in my department the autonomy and flexibility to design lesson plan templates that make sense to them. No wonder he's frustrated with me and not turning in his plans."

A grade-level chair might now say: "Ah ha, that's why Carol asks everyone else in grade-level meetings what they are teaching and never offers up her own opinion or shares what she is doing with us—she's a socializing learner who is feeling out what others are doing."

This does not mean that these leaders are letting Tom off the hook to not turn in lesson plans, or not asking Carol to share her practice. Rather, it means looking for patterns and explanations so that an instructional leader knows how teachers learn and how the structures and leadership she enacts will be both helpful and challenging for her colleagues. There are going to be times when the school's learning agenda challenges and frustrates particular learners. Table 6.1 is a reminder that the things some people will appreciate and find supportive are the very same things that others will dislike and find frustrating.

AT THE END OF THE DAY: THE CRITICAL ROLE OF LEADERSHIP

The leader, teachers, and school need a vision for the school's learning and strategies to realize that vision. In their important longitudinal study of schools in Chicago, Bryk and his colleagues (2010) identified five essential

Table 6.1. Responses to Different Leadership Stances

Leadership Stance	Some people will really like . . .	And others will find it frustrating because . . .
Instrumental	Clear procedures, processes, and tasks	It's too constricting and confining, there's no room for our opinions, what's the purpose anyway?
Socializing	Asking teachers for their opinions and involving others in developing plans and procedures	We don't know where she stands on things, she always asks us to come up with plans but that's her job, why can't we just teach?
Self-Authoring	Pursuing the big questions and always looking for the purpose in things	We want clear plans and tasks, everything is so complicated, none of this seems practical.

school supports: a coherent instructional guidance system, the professional capacity of the faculty, strong parent–community–school ties, a student-centered learning climate, and leadership that drives change. Leaders who figured out what needed to change and how to drive that change saw results in student learning. Instructional leaders have to make sure there is a focus with goals, processes, and support—and then they have to design, lead, and participate.

Jennifer says: "It's very clear to me that a school can't get far beyond where the principal is. If you think that instrumental learning initiatives are not providing the kind of learning the school needs, then it is the leader's job to move the group to another level of learning. When you keep asking those questions, that is the only way that the group will move. The leader plays the role to ask the hard questions, to push the group, when the group might not be able to do so itself."

BEFORE LEAVING THE DESIGN FOR LEARNING DISCUSSION: POTENTIAL PITFALLS

Leaders who have shared their stories with us have helped us to identify potential pitfalls. These pitfalls are not unique to leadership for adult learning, and we recognize that they likely are challenges instructional leaders have already considered. However, having a list of reminders can be helpful when setting off to design and eventually implement.

Pitfall 1: Not identifying who you are as a learner and what that means for your leadership. Knowing who you are as a learner—instrumental, socializing, or self-authoring—and anticipating what that means for your leadership will help you as you design for school learning.

Pitfall 2: Getting confused about where you are in your school learning efforts. If you are working to build the school's instrumental learning, be clear about that with yourself, in your design, and as you share your goals with others. It can get complicated—especially with diverse adult learners in the school who will not all be happy. Being focused and communicating that focus will help others to understand the goals and processes.

Pitfall 3: Working alone. Leaders need other people to diagnose, design, and troubleshoot with. Work with your leadership team, teachers in your school, colleagues in other schools who are attempting similar initiatives, or those who have been successful doing something you want to try. Consult with instrumental, socializing, and self-authoring learners to anticipate where support can be built in. Not only can these colleagues help you to design, but they also can encourage you and help you to "stay the course" when things get messy—which they will.

Pitfall 4: Starting beyond teachers' and the school's learning capacity. All leaders want their schools to be transformative, equitable, and meaningful places for students and teachers to learn. This might lead them to think about implementing learning experiences "beyond" the school's developmental capacity, for example, looking to self-authoring structures because they have the potential to transform teacher practice and student learning. Jumping into critical friends groups, a self-authoring approach described in Chapter 4, in a school that has not experienced self-authoring or even socializing learning, will be challenging. So while leaders attempt these "noble efforts" (Drago-Severson, 2009) for the anticipated learning benefits, or because they do not want to be perceived as underestimating their teachers, this kind of overreach should be avoided.

Pitfall 5: Not being inclusive in determining what a school needs to learn. In schools, like in classrooms, the activity and pace sometimes can be dominated by a few. There often will be frustrated and dissenting teachers, along with others who may be doing exceedingly well who frequently and perhaps loudly will vocalize their feelings. It then becomes important to get feedback from and listen to a broad range of teachers when designing and especially when assessing the progress of a school's learning initiative. Kathy describes being "shocked when my school's organizational health data indicated that 'morale' was one of the strongest organizational health dimensions in the results—it made me realize that I had been relying too heavily on the perspectives of few teachers who frequently shared their ongoing concerns with me rather than listening to more voices."

Pitfall 6: Thinking only short term. Developing school learning takes time. Think "continual" and "continuous." There may be a temptation—or pressure—to seek some immediate improvement for student learning. Karen Louis (2006) explains that "starting with short-term wins is useful in getting people's attention, but these must be woven into a longer saga of change in which the work is never done" (pp. 485–486). Or, as Jennifer put it, "If you are going to believe that adults are going to learn, that they have the capacity to move on and grow, then there is not a switch to turn on; it takes time."

Pitfall 7: Don't check your swing. This has two connotations. Leaders have to take some swings, even if they don't always hit the sweet spot. And once in the process, they have to swing and follow through, and learn from whatever happens. As Jennifer recommends, have faith in the process and trust the structures.

Pitfall 8: Not being clear about who you are and what you stand for. Leaders are in a position to exert leadership. This is one of the most critical leadership acts—to lead for a school's learning. Jennifer says, "We are responsible for all kids' learning in the school—and not just say it but mean it." As Bryk and colleagues (2010) found, in the cases of successful school reform in the Chicago schools, there was *evident leadership*, "a deliberate orchestration of people, programs, and extant resources." Instructional leaders were "not reticent about using their role authority to 'make things happen'" (pp. 62–63).

THE WORK IS NEVER DONE

Leaders have to "make things happen." The way learning leaders do that is by working to make school learning happen. They know that when teachers and the school are learning, students are learning. They also know that this requires the leader's participation and learning. Building one's leadership for learning takes more than time and experience—it requires being a learning leader. Leaders who are willing to look at their own ongoing learning and the complexity of this work have an opportunity to model what it means to be a learner. This is ongoing, continual, and continuous work at all three levels—personal, teacher, and school. Being a learning leader highlights ongoing adult learning on an individual and personal level, to affirm that the work is never done because the learning is never done.

CHAPTER 7

Leading for Learning

Schools where kids learn need to be schools where everyone learns. This simple idea is the fundamental premise of the preceding six chapters. While the idea that everyone in schools needs to learn sounds straightforward enough, the work of supporting student, teacher, and whole-school learning is a complex leadership task. It requires instructional leaders to think broadly about adult learning and have a repertoire of strategies that can be used to support that learning. Like students, adults learn in complex ways that are dependent on a variety of factors.

Throughout this book, we use the lens of constructive-developmental theory and the categories of instrumental, socializing, and self-authoring learning to describe a number of strategies and formats that leaders can use to support the wide range of learning that schools require. Constructive-developmental theory suggests that instrumental learners search for the "right way" to do something and are most comfortable with concrete process and specific answers. Instrumental learners have little interest in collaboration, other perspectives, or self-reflection until their own learning needs are met. Socializing knowers, on the other hand, learn by considering others' viewpoints, working in groups, and reflecting on their practice. Groups are essential for socializing learners; however, they can be uncomfortable taking a stand in opposition to the group or with the conflict that differing opinions and values can generate. Self-authoring learners can be reflective about both themselves and the groups to which they belong. They also can live with ambiguity and tolerate conflict in groups, especially if it is in the service of their own values and principles.

We argue both that there is a complex relationship among these categories of learning and that learning leaders need to be skilled at figuring out what learning their school needs and its capacity for carrying it out. However connected, these three categories of learning are not the same. Each one contains a different set of assumptions about schools and leads to a different place in the work of making schools better places for student learning. In this final chapter, we consider the unique implications of each category of adult learning for the work of improving and transforming schools, and for the work of school leaders.

We propose that an instructional leader who takes an instrumental approach to the work of school reform will work in a very different way and with different goals than a learning leader who takes a socializing or self-authoring approach. Not only will their goals and methods be different, but they will be faced with very different challenges. In this chapter, to help sort out the complexities of thinking about a learning-focused leadership practice, we ask three questions about these approaches to school reform: (1) What are the three approaches and what do they look like? (2) What difference does it make to look at the work of school reform in these ways? (3) What do leaders have to do to develop a learning-focused leadership practice?

THE THREE APPROACHES TO SCHOOL REFORM

The Instrumental Approach to School Reform

The Benefits of the Instrumental Approach

It seems that our nation's schools are always at a crossroads. And these types of crossroads seem to be coming at increasingly alarming rates. The crossroads, for example, may have to do with the choices schools need to make about new literacy programs, or ways to help students think mathematically, or options around dropout prevention strategies. There is no end in sight. Moreover, there is increasing pressure on schools to make exactly the "right" choices when they are at a crossroads. Given the evidence that students do not perform well enough on standardized tests, not enough schools make "adequate yearly progress," students do not fare well in international comparisons, and too many students are not finishing high school, there is considerable pressure on instructional leaders to find the "best" answers and concrete processes that will resolve these many issues. There is considerable pressure for instrumental learning.

In many cases, schools, and even school districts, have become like the instrumental learners in our imaginary school in our imaginary hallway from Chapter 1. Like the teacher who is so overwhelmed that he needs to know—right now—exactly the right way to line students up for lunch, or to teach phonics, or to keep students engaged in a block schedule, school leaders are desperate to find exactly the right literacy program, or social studies curriculum, or dropout prevention strategy. And to find it as quickly as possible.

Schools that take a primarily instrumental approach to the work of school improvement move from one instrumental crossroads to the next. They start with the new math text, then the updated science initiative, then the anti-bullying curriculum, and then the most recent professional development plan. If instrumental learning is a quest for the new best answer and concrete process, then schools and school districts often behave like instrumental learners.

Districts, schools, teams, and departments rely on an instrumental approach for lots of good reasons. Publishers, professional development providers, universities, and researchers have lots of "best answers" for schools—and many of them have merit. And the best answer is often the easiest and most readily available answer as well.

The instrumental path is familiar, well lit, and well traveled. It requires teachers, groups, and schools to learn and implement a new program that most likely has been chosen by someone else. Often, the program is well articulated, comes with lots of resources, is based on some research, and has political support. Moreover, teachers can be held accountable for the degree of fidelity with which they implement what they have learned. The instrumental approach to school reform is a clear and often traveled road. It can be easy to take.

The Limits of the Instrumental Approach

While instrumental learners and instrumental districts and schools share many characteristics, the limits to that approach also are shared. Teachers who are instrumental learners, for example, focus on their own classrooms and their own practice without regard for how students travel through the school or district. However, as students move from one class to another and from one grade to another, it is important that the journey makes sense, that there are connections, and that what happens in one class is related to what happens in other classes (Bryk et al., 2010; Elmore, 2004). And yet, instrumental learning is all about what happens in each teacher's own class.

I've come to the conclusion that you can expect anywhere from 20% to 40% of the studies in any given area to report negative results. While this might surprise or even discourage some, that's simply the nature of the social sciences, in which there are a wide variety of variables that determine whether a particular strategy is going to produce positive results in any given situation. The lesson to be learned is that educators must always look to whether a particular strategy is producing the desired results as opposed to simply assuming that if a strategy is being used, positive results will ensue.

Marzano, 2009, p. 30

The instrumental learning approach to school reform has two significant limits. First, many theorists remind us that the best practice is almost always a "better practice" (Mezirow, 2000). Statistically, the best practice may have a better chance to make a difference than some other practice, but it is never a certainty. The schools that take an instrumental learning approach are drawn to the most accessible, easy answer, to the hope that a best practice inevitably will achieve a desired result if implemented properly. The dilemma, of course, is that there are no easy answers and few statistical certainties in schools.

Second, the instrumental approach, because it focuses on finding the "right answer," often ignores context. Robert Marzano (2009), who has advocated extensively for "high yield" best practice, reminds us: "We also cautioned that research indicates that the instructional strategies we identified might have a positive effect on student achievement in some situations, but have a negligible or even negative effect on student achievement in other situations" (p. 30). His advice to teachers? "Teachers should rely on their knowledge of their students, their subject matter, and their situations to identify the most appropriate instructional strategies" (p. 30).

Context makes a difference, and how the best practice looks in one classroom might, and probably should, be different from how it looks in another classroom, or another school, or another district. Students are different in every classroom: They speak different languages at home, they learn in different ways, their ethnicities vary, they wear different clothes, some have beautiful homes, and some have no home at all. Context makes the easy, best answer a more complicated, tentative answer. Instrumental learners, and instrumental schools, struggle with the complications that taking context into account brings to the work of finding the best answer.

Using the lens of adult learning, it is possible to argue that taking only an instrumental approach might very well limit the progress schools can make in truly improving their practice. The journey from one best practice to the next best practice ignores the complexities of context and the need for coherence. Our adult-learning lens suggests schools might get stuck because the learning needed to solve the dilemmas of context and coherence is socializing learning—learning that is more reflective, understands the perspectives of others, and can build a more coherent vision of teaching and learning across a school and district.

The Socializing Approach to School Reform

The Benefits of the Socializing Approach

If the instrumental approach to school reform is about implementing a best practice as a way of improving individual practice, then the socializing learning approach is about improving everyone's practice in a way that (1) takes into account the specific context in which the practice is enacted, and (2) builds a coherent, schoolwide vision of teaching and learning. Whereas the instrumental approach asks teachers to focus primarily on improving their own classroom, the socializing learning approach to school reform understands that context is critically important and that the best practice is always the better practice. The socializing learning approach, therefore, is not only about fidelity of implementation; it is about adjusting the best practice to fit the particular context in which it is embedded. The socializing approach asks teachers to think about their practice and the difference it makes in their own school and with their own students.

A socializing learning approach to school reform also recognizes that coherence is important for school improvement. Research suggests that student learning can be limited, even in a school full of skilled teachers, if the school does not possess a coherent approach to the work of teaching and learning (Bryk et al., 2010; Elmore, 2004). The socializing learning approach asks teachers to look beyond their own classroom to the complicated, multiyear journeys that students take through any school or school district. Does what happens in 2nd grade support what students need to learn in 3rd grade? Does the district's vision of teaching and learning make sense as students move from middle to high school? The socializing learning approach is similar to the instrumental approach in that they are both concerned with improving teaching practice. However, the socializing approach also asks educators to think about the connections between everyone's practice, take into account the difference that context makes, and build a coherent vision of learning.

Schools, districts, teams, and departments are drawn to a socializing learning approach to school reform because it offers a way to overcome the powerful pull of the forces of conservatism, isolation, and presentism (Hargreaves & Shirley, 2009; Lortie, 1975) that are still found in many schools. By sharing practice, focusing on student learning, and building a shared understanding of teaching, schools begin to overcome these cultural barriers in ways that can improve teacher practice and increase student learning.

The Limits of the Socializing Approach

Educators accustomed to working alone on the current best answer in ways they have always worked do not always have the skills needed for socializing learning. The socializing learning approach to school reform requires educators to learn new ways of working together. Teachers, principals, schools, and districts need to learn how to collaborate, be reflective, focus on teaching and learning, and deprivatize their practice for the sake of their students. And, it is the job of instructional leaders to lead this learning.

A socializing learning approach to school improvement can surface multiple layers of anxiety because it requires teachers to question their assumptions about what it means to be a teacher. In many places, being a teacher means working alone with one's own students, being accountable mainly to a principal who visits infrequently, having minimal professional dialogue, developing one's own lessons, and implementing a reading or math program as one sees fit. Little (1990) describes the actuality of teachers' work by noting, "Observers (including teachers) tend to agree that classroom independence punctuated by occasional contacts among colleagues is the modal reality" (p. 513).

The socializing learning approach challenges educators to redefine themselves to be more public learners who question and share their practice and consider the perspectives of others. Edgar Schein (2010) names the anxiety that typically accompanies such a challenge "survival anxiety" because it requires that educators abandon their current professional identity in favor of an identity that is untried and certainly unfamiliar. The socializing learning approach can surface survival anxiety in a way that instrumental learning does not. Instrumental learning requires only the faithful adoption of the current best answer. Socializing learning asks educators to let go of their instrumental identity as educators and assume one that is untried, uncomfortable, and, as a result, anxiety-producing.

Moreover, socializing learning can engender what Schein (2010) calls "learning anxiety." Not only does the socializing learning approach ask teachers to rethink their identities as teachers, but it also requires them to learn often unfamiliar practices of collaborating, surfacing and questioning assumptions, and making work public. The socializing approach asks educators not only to give up their long-standing, comfortable identities, but also to learn a variety of new, challenging, and complicated practices. For many adults, the socializing approach can produce high levels of both survival and learning anxiety. Rethinking their identity as teachers, questioning their practice in public ways, and constantly learning new practices, can overwhelm teachers who have worked comfortably for years in schools where isolationism, conservatism, and presentism are the norm.

The socializing learning approach to school reform is very much about improving the practice of schools, districts, teams, and departments. This approach encourages teachers to learn from one another, be reflective, consider other perspectives, and build a shared understanding of teaching and learning that takes their own context into account. However, instructional leaders who take a socializing learning approach to school reform, like teachers who are socializing knowers, can find it difficult to ask the "hard questions about purposes and possibilities" of the group to which they belong and about which they care so much (Heifetz, 1994, p. 252). The socializing approach, which can avoid questions that challenge the purpose of schooling, equitable educational practice, or the taken-for-granted norms values and practices that define our schools, can support school improvement, but it stops short of school transformation. The learning that challenges fundamental assumptions, values, and practices, and supports school transformation is self-authoring.

The Self-Authoring Approach to School Reform

The Benefits of the Self-Authoring Approach

Like the socializing approach, the self-authoring approach to school reform recognizes that schools need a learning vision and teaching practice that is coherent and context-driven. The socializing learning approach to school improvement asks educators to build a coherent vision of teaching and learning that improves teaching practice and ensures that student learning is supported at high levels throughout students' journey through schools. This is important and difficult work that undoubtedly makes a difference in student learning. Yet this approach can easily avoid the hardest questions about our schools, the very questions that will need to be answered if we are to truly transform them. The hardest questions require self-authoring learning.

The self-authoring approach is based on the premise that in order to transform schools, educators need to persistently question every school's learning vision and the effects of context on its teaching practice. Self-authoring learning is transformational learning that "focuses on how we learn to negotiate and act on our own purposes, values, feelings, and meanings rather than those we have uncritically assimilated from others" (Mezirow, 2000, p. 8). Self-authoring learning asks and holds on to difficult and unsettling questions.

The self-authoring approach to school reform challenges educators' deeply held beliefs about our practice, our context, and the coherence of our vision of teaching and learning. Self-authoring learning, for example, asks, "What is the purpose of the journey that children take through our schools?" The self-authoring approach wonders whether schools are designed to reinvent or reproduce our society. It asks why so many students are pushed out of our schools. The self-authoring approach challenges us to think not only about context and the challenges that so many of our students face, but also about the context of privilege in which many White, middle-class educators work. The self-authoring approach asks educators, for example, to think about the difference that race, privilege, and class make in individual and schoolwide practice.

> If you do not question your own and the group's preferred interpretation, you and your organization may end up colluding in avoiding the difficult work of addressing the more important issues.
>
> Heifetz, Grashow, and Linsky, 2009, p. 34

The learning that will not only improve schools but also transform them is self-authoring learning, because the work of transforming schools is directly connected to uncomfortable conversations about unequal, unproductive practices and conditions in districts, schools, and classrooms (Singleton & Linton, 2006). Like self-authoring learners, the self-authoring approach to school reform is capable of challenging uncritically accepted assumptions about school context and practice. The self-authoring approach asks educators to tolerate the ambiguity and complexity that come with asking challenging questions about the purpose of schools, the nature of equitable practice, the impact of context, and the implications of coherence.

The answers to important questions about the purpose of schooling require more than either instrumental or socializing learning. There are no specific answers or concrete processes that the instrumental learner seeks. Nor will the answers to these questions be found in the group, as the socializing learner would like. This learning requires all of the skills of instrumental and socializing learning, plus a willingness to expect and accept conflict, and the ability to at times stand in opposition to the group. These are characteristics of self-authoring learners.

The Challenges of the Self-Authoring Approach

The self-authoring approach is clearly the most challenging, and most uncommon, of these learning approaches to school reform. The self-authoring approach heightens the survival anxiety that educators face when they consider the demands on schools to educate students for the 21st century, or the numbers of students who do not finish high school, or the achievement gaps among different groups, or the struggles of kids who speak a different language at home. Heifetz and colleagues (2009) suggest that the self-authoring approach also increases learning anxiety because it asks educators to question their familiar ways of understanding their practice, and their comfortable explanations. This approach challenges teachers not only to learn new and unidentified ways of teaching, of working with one another, and of being in school, but also to create those new ways. The self-authoring approach requires comfort with conflict, the ability to take a principled position, and the willingness to stand in opposition to important groups.

If the instrumental approach is the search for the "best answer," and the socializing approach is the quest for the "better answer," then the self-authoring approach is the pursuit of the "right questions": the questions that will transform a department, team, school, or district.

The self-authoring approach places an intimidating set of demands on instructional leaders. If self-authoring learning is about accepting conflict, tolerating ambiguity, questioning fundamental assumptions about context, searching for the right questions, and resisting the best answers, then the leadership practice of instructional leaders needs to embody these characteristics. This uncommon leadership practice acknowledges that every leader needs to be a learner, that most leadership problems can be thought of as learning problems, and that leadership can—and should—come from anywhere in the school. The self-authoring approach understands that leading and learning are not separate activities.

The self-authoring approach also challenges leaders not only to support others in embracing ambiguity and discomfort, but to tolerate it themselves; not only to support others in transforming their practice, but to transform their own practice; not only to support others in considering fundamental questions about the purpose of schooling, but to raise them for themselves. The self-authoring approach asks leaders to be learners, and to do their learning in a public and transparent way.

The irony for instructional leaders in taking a self-authoring approach is that the competencies that helped them be successful in leading instrumental and socializing learners are no longer as useful. The self-authoring approach asks leaders not to be the "learning expert" that they are in the instrumental approach, or to be the "process expert" and facilitator of the group, as the socializing approach requires. The self-authoring approach asks leaders to become members of the group and to be learners themselves. For instructional leaders, the increased survival and learning anxiety, the search for the right questions rather than easy answers, and the rethinking of what it means to be a leader are all factors that make the self-authoring approach the most challenging of our three approaches. Yet this most difficult of approaches is also the one whose goal is the transformation of schools.

WHY A LEARNING APPROACH TO SCHOOL LEADERSHIP

So what difference does it make to look at schools through the lens of adult learning? School leaders are already expected to be prudent fiscal agents, effective communicators, canny politicians, capable consensus builders, instructional experts, child advocates, rigorous followers of bureaucratic regulation, and many, many other things. Does "leader of teacher learning" have to be added to this list? So what is a leader's work in schools? Not surprisingly, in our view, there is an instrumental, a socializing, and a self-authoring answer to these questions—and they are all different.

The instrumental leader's approach to school reform is to quickly respond to these questions by admitting that, indeed, "being a leader of adult learning" needs to be on the list of what a leader's work is. Yes, the instrumental leader says, "To improve schools, leaders need to manage the budget, advocate for children, faithfully implement district and state regulations, be an effective supervisor, *and also* lead adult learning." For instrumental leaders, leading learning for school professionals is another concrete, best answer to the question of what a leader's work is. Instrumental leaders have a long list and make heroic efforts to ensure that every item on the list is fully addressed.

The socializing approach to school reform answers our "so what" questions by saying that leading adult learning cannot simply be another item on the leader's job description. Because socializing leaders are concerned with building a coherent, shared vision of schooling, they understand that a leader's work needs also to be coherent and grounded in context. The socializing leader understands that the long list of tasks and competencies that make up a leader's work needs to make sense. Tasks such as following regulations, building budgets, advocating for kids, and paying attention to political forces need to support the work of building a collaborative, reflective community built on a shared understanding of teaching and learning. Socializing leaders build schoolwide professional communities by making leading adult learning the heart of their practice.

On the other hand, the self-authoring approach responds to the questions about the nature of a leader's work not with a different answer, but with some difficult questions. The self-authoring leader asks the instrumental leader, "Why is *this* the list of expectations for school leaders? Who assembles it? Who benefits from thinking in this way about leadership? Who does not?" The self-authoring leader asks the socializing leader, "Whose voices are included in building a coherent vision of schooling, and whose are left out? What is the purpose of schools? Whose children are served by that vision? Whose are not?" The self-authoring leader answers our questions about leading adult learning by modeling what self-authoring learning is all about: She asks the hard questions.

For the instrumental leader, leading adult learning is a task to be put on the list of ways to improve individual classroom practice—and she is right. The socializing leader thinks of leading adult learning as the way that schools work together to build a coherent vision of teaching and learning that improves teaching and learning schoolwide—and he is right.

The self-authoring leader thinks that leading adult learning is about taking up the most challenging issues in a public and transparent way in order to transform schools—and she is also right. They are all right, but not all of the time or in every place.

Looking at schools through the lens of adult learning changes an instructional leader's understanding of what a leader's work is and how it is carried out. The instrumental leader thinks that the work of leading adult learning is one of many tasks that need to be accomplished. The socializing leader thinks that leading is about building a coherent schoolwide professional community. The self-authoring leader thinks that leadership is asking difficult questions about the purpose of schools, exposing closely held assumptions about teaching and learning, and surfacing issues of equitable educational practice.

The lens of adult learning also changes what instructional leaders think their work is (see Table 7.1). For instrumental leaders, the adult-learning lens suggests that the work of leaders is to improve individual practice. Socializing leaders understand that their work is to improve the practice of the entire school. Their work is school improvement, not just individual teacher improvement. Self-authoring leaders understand their work to be the transformation of schools. Their work is not just to improve but to transform what happens in schools.

Table 7.1. Leadership Approaches to School Reform

Leader's Approach	Leader's Work	How Leader Leads
Instrumental	Improve individual classroom practice	Content expert: leading adult learning is one of many leadership tasks
Socializing	Whole-school improvement by building collaborative, reflective, learning-focused school communities	Process expert: persistent focus on building a shared vision of good practice and powerful learning grounded in context of school; leading adult learning is at the center of leadership practice
Self-Authoring	School transformation: build capacity to address complex issues of equitable educational practice, question fundamental assumptions, and expect and accept discomfort	Leads adult learning by learning in a public and transparent way: willing to raise uncomfortable questions about own practice, learn in public ways, and resist easy answers

HOW TO LEAD EDUCATOR LEARNING

So, if how we lead educator learning makes a difference in our leadership practice, now what do we need in order to get better at such a learning-focused leadership practice? Again the answer seems complicated—but it is not. A leader needs three qualities: purpose, eagerness for learning, and courage.

Purpose is important because learning leaders need to be clear about the learning their teams, departments, schools, or districts need. Some schools need instrumental learning, others socializing learning, and a few are ready for self-authoring learning. An instructional leader is effective when he understands, for example, that self-authoring learning will not flourish in a school that is only beginning to acquire the skills of socializing learning. Similarly, school transformation is not likely to happen in a school where instrumental learning about classroom practice has never happened. Effective learning leaders need to be very purposeful about the learning they lead and how they lead it.

Learning leaders need to be eager to learn. If schools become better places for children when adults learn, it is also true that schools become better places for adults to learn when leaders learn. Teachers will not learn in the public, collaborative way that it takes to improve practice schoolwide if the learning leader does not do the same. This means that a leader needs to be not only willing to learn, but also eager to learn in a public, transparent, and risky way. It's not easy.

Finally, learning in a public and transparent way takes courage, especially for leaders who typically are expected to solve problems, provide answers, and give direction—courage to raise unsettling questions, courage to expose and explore what they do not know, courage to accept ambiguity, and courage to embrace discomfort. Leading adult learning takes courage because this leadership succeeds only when the leader is also a learner.

Now what? The "now what" is to build learning capacity for the transformation of schools, and for school leadership that is more purposeful, more eager for learning, and more courageous. The more leaders learn, the more adults learn, the better places schools are for our children to learn.

The Collaborative Assessment Conference *Protocol*

1. Getting Started

- The group chooses a facilitator who will make sure the group stays focused on the particular issue addressed in each step.
- The presenting teacher puts the selected work in a place where everyone can see it or provides copies for the other participants. S/he says nothing about the work, the context in which it was created, or the student, until Step 5.
- The participants observe or read the work in silence, perhaps making brief notes about aspects of it that they particularly notice.

2. Describing the Work

- The facilitator asks the group, "What do you see?"
- Group members provide answers without making judgments about the quality of the work or their personal preferences.
- If a judgment emerges, the facilitator asks for the evidence on which the judgment is based.

3. Asking Questions About the Work

- The facilitator asks the group, "What questions does this work raise for you?"
- Group members state any questions they have about the work, the child, the assignment, the circumstances under which the work was carried out, and so on.
- The presenting teacher may choose to make notes about these questions, but s/he does not respond to them now—nor is s/he obligated to respond to them in Step 5 during the time s/he speaks.

4. Speculating About What the Student Is Working on

- The facilitator asks the group, "What do you think the child is working on?"
- Participants, based on their reading or observation of the work, make suggestions about the problems or issues that the student might have been focused on in carrying out the assignment.

5. Hearing from the Presenting Teacher

- The facilitator invites the presenting teacher to speak.
- The presenting teacher provides his/her perspective on the student's work, describing what s/he sees in it, responding (if s/he chooses) to one or more of the questions raised, and adding any other information that s/he feels is important to share with the group.
- The presenting teacher also comments on anything surprising or unexpected that s/he heard during the describing, questioning, and speculating phases.

6. Discussing Implications for Teaching and Learning

- The facilitator invites everyone (the participants and the presenting teacher) to share any thoughts they have about their own teaching, children's learning, or ways to support this particular child in future instruction.

7. Reflecting on the Collaborative Assessment Conference

- The group reflects on the experiences of the conference as a whole or to particular parts of it.

8. Thanks to the Presenting Teacher

NOTE

The *Collaborative Assessment Conference* Protocol was developed by Steve Seidel. The protocol and more information are available at http://schoolreforminitiative. org/doc/cac.pdf

The Tuning *Protocol*

1. Introduction (5 minutes)

- Facilitator briefly introduces protocol goals, guidelines, and process
- Participants briefly introduce themselves

2. Presentation (15 minutes)

The presenter has an opportunity to share the context for the student work:

- Information about the students and/or the class—what the students tend to be like, where they are in school, where they are in the year
- Assignment or prompt that generated the student work
- Student learning goals or standards that inform the work
- Samples of student work—photocopies of work, video clips, and so on—with student names removed
- Evaluation format—scoring rubric and/or assessment criteria, and so on
- Focusing question for feedback

3. Clarifying Questions (5 minutes)

- Participants have an opportunity to ask clarifying questions in order to get information that may have been omitted in the presentation that they feel would help them to understand the context for the student work. Clarifying questions are matters of fact.
- The facilitator should be sure to limit the questions to those that are clarifying, judging which questions more properly belong in the warm/cool feedback section.

4. Examination of Student Work Samples (15 minutes)

- Participants look closely at the work, taking notes on where it seems to be in tune with the stated goals, and where there might be a problem. Participants focus particularly on the presenter's focusing question.
- Presenter is silent; participants do this work silently.

5. Pause to Reflect on Warm and Cool Feedback (2–3 minutes)

- Participants take a couple of minutes to reflect on what they would like to contribute to the feedback session.
- Presenter is silent; participants do this work silently.

6. Warm and Cool Feedback (15 minutes)

- Participants share feedback with one another while the presenter is silent. The feedback begins with a few minutes of warm feedback, moves on to a few minutes of cool feedback (sometimes phrased in the form of reflective questions), and then moves back and forth between warm and cool feedback.
- Warm feedback may include comments about how the work presented seems to meet the desired goals; cool feedback may include possible disconnects, gaps, or problems. Often participants offer ideas or suggestions for strengthening the work presented.
- The facilitator may need to remind participants of the presenter's focusing question, which should be posted for all to see.
- Presenter is silent and takes notes.

7. Reflection (5 minutes)

- Presenter speaks to those comments/questions s/he chooses while participants are silent.
- This is not a time to defend oneself, but is instead a time for the presenter to reflect aloud on those ideas or questions that seemed particularly interesting.
- Facilitator may intervene to focus, clarify, and so on.

8. Debrief (5 minutes)

- Facilitator-led discussion of this tuning experience.

NOTE

The *Tuning* Protocol was originally developed by Joseph McDonald and the Coalition of Essential Schools Exhibitions Project, and further developed by David Allen. Retrieved from http://schoolreforminitiative.org/doc/tuning.pdf

The Consultancy *Protocol*

A *Consultancy* is a structured process for helping an individual or a team think more expansively about a particular, concrete dilemma. Outside perspective is critical for this protocol to work effectively; therefore, some of the participants in the group must be people who do not share the presenter's specific dilemma at that time. When putting together a *Consultancy* group, be sure to include people with differing perspectives.

Time: Approximately 50 minutes

Roles

Presenter (whose work is being discussed by the group)
Facilitator (who sometimes participates, depending on the size of the group)

Protocol

1. The presenter gives an overview of the dilemma with which s/he is struggling, and frames a question for the *Consultancy* group to consider. The framing of this question, as well as the quality of the presenter's reflection on the dilemma being discussed, are key features of this protocol. If the presenter has brought student work, educator work, or other "artifacts," there is a pause here to silently examine the work/documents. The focus of the group's conversation is on the dilemma. (5–10 minutes)

2. The *Consultancy* group asks clarifying questions of the presenter— that is, questions that have brief, factual answers. (5 minutes)

3. The group asks probing questions of the presenter. These questions should be worded so that they help the presenter clarify and expand his/her thinking about the dilemma presented to the *Consultancy* group. The goal here is for the presenter to learn more about the question s/he framed or to do some analysis of the dilemma

presented. The presenter may respond to the group's questions, but there is no discussion by the *Consultancy* group of the presenter's responses. At the end of the 10 minutes, the facilitator asks the presenter to restate his/her question for the group. (10 minutes)

4. The group members talk with one another about the dilemma presented. (15 minutes)

Possible questions to frame the discussion:

- What did we hear?
- What didn't we hear that we think might be relevant?
- What assumptions seem to be operating?
- What questions does the dilemma raise for us?
- What do we think about the dilemma?
- What might we do or try if faced with a similar dilemma?
- What have we done in similar situations?

Members of the group sometimes suggest actions the presenter might consider taking. Most often, however, they work to define the issues more thoroughly and objectively. The presenter doesn't speak during this discussion, but instead listens and takes notes.

5. The presenter reflects on what s/he heard and on what s/he is now thinking, sharing with the group anything that particularly resonated for him/her during any part of the *Consultancy*. (5 minutes)

6. The facilitator leads a brief conversation about the group's observation of the *Consultancy* process. (5 minutes)

NOTE

The *Consultancy* Protocol was developed by Gene Thompson-Grove, Paula Evans, and Faith Dunne at the School Reform Initiative. Retrieved from http://school reforminitiative.org/doc/consultancy.pdf

APPENDIX D

Establishing Ground Rules

Ground rules, or norms, are important for a group that intends to work together on difficult issues, or that will be working together over time. Ground rules may be added to, or condensed, as the group progresses. Starting with basic ground rules builds trust, clarifies group expectations of one another, and establishes points of "reflection" to see how the group is doing regarding process.

Time: Approximately 30 minutes

1. Ask everyone to **write down what each person needs in order to work productively in a group,** giving an example of one thing the facilitator needs, that is, "to have all voices heard," or "to start and end our meetings when we say we will." (This is to help people focus on process rather than product.)

2. **Have each participant name *one* thing from his/her written list,** going around in a circle, with no repeats, and as many circuits as necessary to have all the ground rules listed.

3. **Ask for any clarifications** needed. One person may not understand what another person has listed, or may interpret the language differently.

4. **If the list is very long—more than 10 ground rules—ask the group if some of them can be combined to make the list more manageable.** Sometimes the subtle differences are important to people, so it is more important that everyone feel their needs have been honored than it is to have a short list.

5. **Ask if everyone can abide by the listed ground rules.** If anyone dislikes or doesn't want to comply with one of them, that ground rule should be discussed and a decision should be made to keep it on the list with a notation of the objection, to remove it, or to try it for a specified amount of time and check it again.

6. **Ask if any of the ground rules might be hard for the group to follow.**
   If there is one or more, those ground rules should be highlighted and
   given attention. With time it will become clear whether it should be
   dropped, or needs significant work. Sometimes what might appear
   to be a difficult rule turns out not to be hard at all. "Everyone has a
   turn to speak," is sometimes debated, for example, with the argument
   that not everyone likes to talk every time an issue is raised, while
   others think aloud and process well only if they have the space to
   do that. Frequently, a system of checking in with everyone, without
   requiring everyone to speak, becomes a more effective ground rule.

7. **While work is in progress, refer to the ground rules whenever
   they would help the group process.** If one person is dominating,
   for example, it is easier to refer to a ground rule that says,
   "take care with how often and how long you speak," than
   to ask someone directly to stop dominating the group.

8. **Check in on the ground rules when reflection is done on the group
   work.** Note any that were not followed particularly well for attention
   in the next work session. Being sure they are followed, refining
   them, and adding or subtracting ground rules is important, as it
   makes for smoother work and more trust within the group.

NOTE

Establishing Ground Rules was developed by Marylyn Wentworth. It can be
retrieved under the title Forming Ground Rules, from http://schoolreforminitiative.
org/doc/forming_ground_rules.pdf

Setting Norms for Collaborative Work

Norms are ways of working together that help groups be more thoughtful and productive. They fall into two categories: procedural and interpersonal. Once norms have been established, it is important that the entire group, not just the facilitator, takes responsibility for making sure that the norms are respected, and for redirecting the group when they are not. Norms can change and evolve as the group develops and matures.

Areas to Consider When Setting Norms

- Logistics: meeting time, place, duration, and frequency
- Timeliness: start time, finish time, lateness, and attendance
- Courtesy: listening, interruptions, equal participation, dealing with disagreements, respect, empathy, and sharing the workload
- Decision-making process: How will we make decisions? Reach agreements? How will we show agreement?
- Workload assignment: How will work be assigned? How will conflicts with existing workloads be settled?
- Setting priorities: How will we discharge responsibility for on-time completion and equal distribution?
- Enforcement of norms: How will we make sure the norms are followed?

Activity for Setting Norms

1. The facilitator passes out four to six Post-it® notes to each team member.

2. All group members write a norm (a statement about how they want the group to work together) on the note. Each note should contain only one norm.

3. The team shares its individual notes and divides them into the two categories—procedural norms and interpersonal norms.

4. Within each category, similar suggestions are grouped (e.g., "take turns speaking" and "make sure everyone speaks" would be grouped together).

5. A name is given to the norm formed from each group of similar suggestions. (From the example above, the norm could be, "Make sure everyone is heard.")

6. The group discusses the norms that have been suggested and checks to see whether members are in agreement. The group should reach consensus on the ones it accepts.

Hints:

- The team will work with greater commitment if it generates its norms itself.
- Display the norms during each meeting.
- Add new norms as the team develops and new situations arise.

NOTE

For more information on Setting Norms for Collaborative Work, visit http://www.scoe.org/files/setting-norms.pdf

APPENDIX F

Resources

Chapter 2: Instrumental Learning in Schools

Study Groups: Along with texts mentioned in the chapter, Learning Forward, formerly the National Staff Development Council (www. learningforward.org), has developed resources and experiences to help instructional leaders design and implement study groups. Murphy and Lick (2006) have developed a fieldbook for developing study groups called *The Whole-Faculty Study Groups Fieldbook: Lessons Learned and Best Practices from Classrooms, Districts, and Schools.*

Walkthroughs: For school leaders interested in doing walkthroughs with a team with a specific focus that is to be reported to a school community, resources include Learning Forward (www.learningforward.org) and the Institute for Learning at the University of Pittsburgh (http://ifl. lrdc.pitt.edu/ifl/). Harvard Graduate School of Education provides seminars regarding instructional rounds (www.gse.harvard.edu/ ppe/programs/prek-12/portfolio/instructional-rounds.html).

Chapter 3: Socializing Learning in Schools

Learning Communities: Learning Forward (www.learningfoward. org), Solution Tree (www.solution-tree.com/Public/Main. aspx), and SEDL (formerly Southwest Educational Development Laboratory; www.sedl.org/) are among the organizations that provide information, resources, and professional learning opportunities related to creating learning communities.

Protocols: The School Reform Initiative (www.schoolreforminitiative.org) offers access to a variety of protocols for learning from text, looking at student and adult work, and conducting observations, including the *Final Word, 4 "A"s Text Protocol, Tuning, Collaborative Assessment Conference, Consultancy, First Classroom Visits,* and *Focus Point.*

Two books that provide extensive examples of the use of protocols are *The Power of Protocols: An Educator's Guide to Better Practice* (McDonald, Mohr, Dichter, & McDonald, 2007) and *Looking Together at Student Work* (Blythe, Allen, & Powell, 2007). Both are available through Teachers College Press (www.tcpress.com).

Chapter 4: Self-Authoring Learning in Schools

Learning About Race and Equity: An online course based on *Courageous Conversations About Race* (Singleton, 2011), as well as other materials and professional development, can be found at http://www.corwin. com/pl/courses/singleton.htm. Other resources are available through the National Equity Project (http://nationalequityproject.org/) and Rethinking Schools (www.rethinkingschools.org/index.shtml).

Lesson Study: Resources such as professional learning opportunities, examples, descriptions, and readings are offered by the Chicago Lesson Study Group (www.lessonstudygroup.net) and the Lesson Study Group at Mills College (www.lessonresearch.net).

Teacher-Led Inquiry: Information about teacher-led inquiry, including examples of ongoing inquiry initiatives, can be found on the website of the National Writing Project (www.nwp.org/cs/public/print/ resource_topic/teacher_research_inquiry) and on the website of Project Zero (http://pzweb.harvard.edu/Research/Evidence.htm).

Chapter 5: How Leaders Facilitate for Learning

Group Facilitation: Sam Kaner and others who wrote *Facilitator's Guide to Participatory Decision-Making* created a website (www. communityatwork.com/index.html) that offers professional learning opportunities, as well as links to other resources and organizations related to facilitative leaderships.

Facilitating Protocols for Learning: As described in the resources for Chapters 2 and 3, the School Reform Initiative (SRI) offers access to a variety of protocols via its website (www.schoolreforminitiative. org) and resource book. SRI also provides professional learning for educators interested in using protocols to improve teaching and learning (www.schoolreforminitiative.org). A book that provides insight and guidance in the facilitation of protocols is *The Facilitator's Book of Questions* (Allen & Blythe, 2004).

Openings Are Important—Two check-in processes include *Open Circle* (http://www.open-circle.org/index.html) and *Connections* (http://schoolreforminitiative.org/protocol/doc/connections.pdf).

Chapter 6: How Leaders Design for Learning

Design Check: Are we listening to others?: Resources to engage students in assessing their own learning can be found on the website for the What Kids Can Do organization (www.whatkidscando.org).

Design Question 3: Who Am I as a Learner and Leader?—Three books referenced in this chapter include several leadership exercises and questionnaires that can help leaders think about who they are and how they operate as a leader. These include *Leadership for Learning* (Glickman, 2002), *SuperVision and Instructional Leadership: A Developmental Approach* (Glickman, Gordon, & Ross-Gordon, 2010), and *Supervision: A Redefinition* (Sergiovanni & Starratt, 2002).

References

Achinstein, B. (2002). Conflict among community: The micropolitics of teacher collaboration. *Teachers College Record, 104*(3), 421–455.

Achinstein, B., & Aguirre, J. (2008). Cultural match or culturally suspect: How new teachers of color negotiate sociocultural challenges in the classroom. *Teachers College Record, 110*(8), 1505–1540.

Allen, D. (Ed.). (1998). *Assessing student learning: From grading to understanding.* New York: Teachers College Press.

Allen, D., & Blythe, T. (2004). *The facilitator's book of questions: Tools for looking together at student and teacher work.* New York: Teachers College Press.

Annenberg Institute for School Reform. (1997). *National School Reform Faculty: Theory and constructs.* Retrieved from http://www.annenberginstitute.org

Argyris, C. (1982). *Reasoning, learning, and action: Individual and organizational.* San Francisco: Jossey-Bass.

Argyris, C. (1999). *On organizational learning.* Malden, MA: Blackwell.

Asia Society International Studies Schools Network. (2011). Retrieved from http://www.asiasociety.org/education/international-studies-schools-network

Behrstock-Sherrat, E., & Coggshall, J. G. (2010). Realizing the promise of generation Y. *Educational Leadership, 67*(8), 28–34.

Birman, B. F., Desimone, L., Porter, A. C., & Garet, M. S. (2000). Designing professional development that works. *Educational Leadership, 57*(8), 28–33.

Bisplinghoff, B. S., & Allen, J. (Eds.). (1998). *Engaging teachers: Creating teaching/researching relationships.* Portsmouth, NH: Heinemann.

Blythe, T., Allen, D., & Powell, B. S. (2007). *Looking together at student work: A companion guide to assessing student learning* (2nd ed.). New York: Teachers College Press.

Bryk, A. S., Sebring, P. S., Allensworth, E., Luppescu, S., & Easton, J. (2010). *Organizing schools for improvement: Lessons from Chicago.* Chicago: University of Chicago Press.

Cervone, L., & Martinez-Miller, P. (2007, Summer). Classroom walkthroughs as a catalyst for school improvement. *Leadership Compass, 4*(4). Retrieved from www.naesp.org/resources/2/Leadership_Compass/2007/LC2007v4n4a2.pdf

Charney, R. S. (1992). *Teaching children to care: Management in the responsive classroom.* Turners Falls, MA: Northeast Foundation for Children.

Chicago Lesson Study Group. (2011). Retrieved from http://www.lessonstudy.net

City, E. A., Elmore, R. F., Fiarman, S. E., & Teitel, L. (2009). *Instructional rounds in education.* Cambridge, MA: Harvard Education Press.

Cochran-Smith, M. (2002). Learning and unlearning: The education of teacher educators. *Teachers and Teacher Education, 19,* 5–28.

Collaborative Assessment Conference. (n.d.). Retrieved from http://www.school reform.org/protocol/cac.pdf

College Board. (2011). Retrieved from http://www.collegeboard.org

Community at Work. (2011). Retrieved from http://www.communityatwork.com

Consultancy. (n.d.). Retrieved from http://www.schoolreforminitiative.org/protocol/ doc/consultancy.pdf

Costa, A. L., & Kallick, B. (1993). Through the lens of a critical friend. *Educational Leadership, 51* (2), 49–51.

Cushman, K. (2003). *Fires in the bathroom: Advice for teachers from high school students.* New York: New Press.

Cushman, K. (2010). *Fires in the mind: What kids can tell us about motivation and mastery.* San Francisco: Jossey-Bass.

Darling-Hammond, L. (2010). *The flat world and education: How America's commitment to equity will determine our future.* New York: Teachers College Press.

Donaldson, G. A. (2008). *How leaders learn: Cultivating capacities for school improvement.* New York: Teachers College Press.

Drago-Severson, E. (2008). 4 practices serve as pillars for adult learning. *Journal of Staff Development, 29*(4), 60–63.

Drago-Severson, E. (2009). *Leading adult learning: Supporting adult development in our schools.* Thousand Oaks, CA: Corwin Press.

DuFour, R. (2011, February). Work together but only if you want to. *Kappan,* 57–61.

DuFour, R., & Eaker, R. (1998). *Professional learning communities at work: Best practices for enhancing student achievement.* Bloomington, IN: National Educational Service.

Easton, L. B. (Ed.). (2004). *Powerful designs for professional learning.* Oxford, OH: National Staff Development Council.

Elmore, R. (2004). *School reform from the inside out: Policy, practice, and performance.* Cambridge, MA: Harvard Education Press.

Eubanks, E., Parish, R., & Smith, D. (1997). Changing the discourse in schools. In P. Hall (Ed.), *Race, ethnicity, and multiculturalism* (Missouri Symposium on Research and Educational Policy Series, Vol. 1.) (pp. 151–168). New York: Garland Press.

Fahey, K. (2011). Still learning about leading: A leadership critical friends group. *Journal of Research on Leadership Education, 6*(1), 1–35.

Final Word. (n.d.). Retrieved from http://schoolreforminitiative.org/protocol/doc/ final_word.pdf

First Classroom Visits. (n.d.). Retrieved from http://schoolreforminitiative.org/protocol/doc/first_visits.pdf

Focus Point Protocol. (n.d.). Retrieved from http://schoolreforminitiative.org/protocol/doc/obs_focus_point.pdf

Four "A"s Text Protocol. (2005). Retrieved from http://schoolreforminitiative.org/protocol/doc/4_a_text.pdf

Glickman, C. D. (1993). *Renewing America's schools: A guide for school-based action.* San Francisco: Jossey-Bass.

Glickman, C. D. (2002). *Leadership for learning: How to help teachers succeed.* Alexandria, VA: Association for Supervision and Curriculum Development.

Glickman, C. D., Gordon, S. P., & Ross-Gordon, J. M. (2010). *SuperVision and instructional leadership: A developmental approach* (8th ed.). Boston: Allyn & Bacon.

Guskey, T. R. (1995). Integrating school improvement programs. In J. H. Block, S. T. Everson, & T. R. Guskey (Eds.), *School improvement programs* (pp. 453–472). New York: Scholastic Press.

Guskey, T. R. (2000). *Evaluating professional development* (2nd ed.). Thousand Oaks, CA: Corwin Press.

Guskey, T. R. (2002). Professional development and teacher change. *Teachers and Teaching: Theory and Practice, 8*(3/4), 381–391.

Guskey, T. R., & Yoon, K. S. (2009). What works in professional development? *Phi Delta Kappan, 90*(7), 495–500.

Hargreaves, A., & Shirley, D. (2009). The persistence of presentism. *Teachers College Record, 111*(11), 2505–2534.

Harvard Graduate School of Education. (2011). Retrieved from http://www.gse.harvard.edu/ppe/programs/prek-12/portfolio/instructional-rounds.html

Heifetz, R. (1994). *Leadership without easy answers.* Cambridge, MA: Harvard University Press.

Heifetz, R., Grashow, A., & Linsky, M. (2009). *The practice of adaptive leadership: Tools and tactics for changing your organization and the world.* Cambridge, MA: Harvard Business Press.

Heifetz, R., & Linsky, M. (2002). *Leadership on the line: Staying alive through the dangers of leading.* Cambridge, MA: Harvard Business School Press.

Hoffmann, F., & Johnston, J. H. (2005). Professional development for principals, by principals. *Leadership, 34*(5), 1–19.

Hubbard, R. S., & Power, B. M. (1999). *Living the questions: A guide for teacher researchers.* York, ME: Stenhouse.

Ingersoll, R., & Merrill, L. (2010). Who's teaching our children? *Educational Leadership, 67*(8), 14–20.

Institute for Learning. (2011). Retrieved from http://ifl.lrdc.pitt.edu/ifl/

Johnson, S. M., & Donaldson, M. L. (2007). Overcoming the obstacles to leadership. *Educational Leadership, 65*(1), 8–13.

Johnson, S. M., & the Next Generation of Teachers Project. (2004). *Finders and keepers*. San Francisco: Jossey-Bass.

Kaner, S., Lind, L., Toldi, C., Fisk, S., & Berger, D. (2007). *Facilitator's guide to participatory decision-making* (2nd ed.). San Francisco: Jossey-Bass.

Kee, K., Anderson, K., Dearing, V., Harris, E., & Shuster, F. (2010). *Results coaching: The new essential for school leaders*. Thousand Oaks, CA: Corwin Press.

Kegan, R. (1998). *In over our heads: The mental demands of modern life*. Cambridge, MA: Harvard University Press.

Kegan, R., & Lahey, L. L. (2009). *Immunity to change: How to overcome it and unlock the potential in yourself and your organization*. Boston: Harvard Business School Press.

Knefelcamp, L., & David-Lang, T. (2000, Spring/Summer). Encountering diversity on campus and in the classroom: Advancing intellectual and ethical development. *Diversity Digest*, 10.

Knight, J. (2011). What good coaches do. *Educational Leadership, 69*(2), 18–22.

Kruse, S., Louis, K., & Bryk, A. (1994, Spring). Building professional learning communities in school. *Issues in Restructuring Schools*, Report No. 6, 3–6. Retrieved from http://www.wcer.wisc.edu/archive/cors/issues_in_restructuring_schools/issues_no_6_spring_1994.pdf

Ladson-Billings, G. (2006). Foreword. In G. Singleton & C. Linton, *Courageous conversations about race* (pp. ix–xi). Thousand Oaks, CA: Corwin Press.

Learning Forward. (2011). Retrieved from http://www.learningforward.org

Leithwood, K., Louis, K. S., Anderson, S., & Wahlstrom, K. (2004). *How leadership influences student learning*. Minneapolis: University of Minnesota, Center for Applied Research and Educational Improvement; & Toronto: Ontario Institute for Studies in Education.

Lesson Study Group at Mills College. (2011). Retrieved from http://www.lesson research.net/

Lewis, C., Perry, R., & Hurd, J. (2004). A deeper look at lesson study. *Educational Leadership, 61*(5), 18–22.

Lewis, C., Perry, R., & Hurd, J. (2009). Improving mathematics instruction through lesson study: A theoretical model and North American case. *Journal of Math Teacher Education, 12*(4). Retrieved from http://www.lessonstudygroup.net/lg/reading_table.php

Lewis, C., Perry, R., Foster, D., Hurd, J., & Fisher, L. (2011). Lesson study: Beyond coaching. *Educational Leadership, 69*(2), 64–68.

Lieberman, A., & Friedrich, L. (2010). *How teachers become leaders: Learning from practice and research*. New York: Teachers College Press.

Lieberman, A., & Miller, L. (2008). *Teachers in professional communities: Improving teaching and learning*. New York: Teachers College Press.

Little, J. W. (1990). The persistence of privacy: Autonomy and initiative in teachers' professional relations. *Teachers College Record, 91*(4), 509–536.

Little, J. W. (2003). Inside teacher community: Representations of classroom practice. *Teachers College Record, 105*(6), 913–945.

Lortie, D. C. (1975). *Schoolteacher: A sociological study.* Chicago: University of Chicago Press.

Louis, K. S. (2006). Changing the culture of schools: Professional community, organizational learning, and trust. *Journal of School Leadership, 16,* 477–487.

Lytle, S. L., & Cochran-Smith, M. (1992). Teacher research as a way of knowing. *Harvard Educational Review, 62,* 447–474.

Marzano, R. (2009). Setting the record straight about "high yield" strategies. *Phi Delta Kappan, 9*(1), 30–37.

Marzano, R., Waters, T., & McNulty, T. (2005). *School leadership that works: From research to results.* Alexandria, VA: Association for Supervision and Curriculum Development.

McDonald, J. P. (1993). Three pictures of an exhibition: Warm, cool, and hard. *Phi Delta Kappan, 74*(6), 480–485.

McDonald, J. P., Mohr, N., Dichter, A., & McDonald, E. (2007). *The power of protocols: An educator's guide to better practice* (2nd ed.). New York: Teachers College Press.

McLaughlin, M., & Talbert, J. (2006). *Building school-based teacher learning communities: Strategies to improve student achievement.* New York: Teachers College Press.

Mezirow, J. (2000). *Learning as transformation: Critical perspectives on a theory in progress.* San Francisco: Jossey Bass.

Mitgang, L., & Maeroff, G. (2008). *Becoming a leader: Preparing school principals for today's schools.* New York: Wallace Foundation.

Mohr, M., Rogers, C., Sanford, B., Nocerino, M. A., MacLean, M., & Clawson, S. (2004). *Teacher research for better schools.* New York: Teachers College Press.

Moir, E., Barlin, D., Gless, J., & Miles, J. (2009). *New teacher mentoring: Hopes and promise for improving teacher effectiveness.* Cambridge, MA: Harvard Education Press.

Murphy, C. U. (1992). Study groups foster schoolwide learning. *Educational Leadership, 50*(3), 71–74.

Murphy, C. U., & Lick, D. W. (2004). *Whole-faculty study groups: Professional learning communities that target student learning* (3rd ed.). Thousand Oaks, CA: Corwin Press.

Murphy, C. U., & Lick, D. W. (2006). *The whole-faculty study groups fieldbook: Lessons learned and best practices from classrooms, districts, and schools.* Thousand Oaks, CA: Corwin Press.

National Equity Project. (2011). Retrieved from http://www.nationalequityproject.org

National Writing Project. (2011). Retrieved from http://www.nwp.org

Newmann, F., & Wehlage, G. (1995). *Successful school restructuring.* Madison: Wisconsin Center for Education Research, Center on Organization and Restructuring of Schools.

Open Circle. (n.d.). Retrieved from http://www.open-circle.org/

Pajak, E. (2003). *Honoring diverse teaching styles: A guide for supervisors.* Alexandria, VA: Association for Supervision and Curriculum Development.

Pankake, A., & Moller, G. (2007). What the teacher leader needs from the principal. *Journal of Staff Development, 28*(1), 32–34.

Pollock, M. (2008). *Everyday antiracism: Getting real about race in school.* New York: New Press.

Project Zero. (2011). Retrieved from http://pzweb.harvard.edu/Research/Evidence.htm

Protheroe, N. (2009). Using classroom walkthroughs to improve instruction. *Principal, 88*(4), 30–34.

Responsive Classroom. (2011). Retrieved from http://www.responsiveclassroom.org/

Rethinking Schools. (2011). Retrieved from http://www.rethinkingschools.org

Robbins, P. (1999, Summer). Mentoring. *Journal of Staff Development, 20*(3), 40–42.

Schein, E. (2010). *Organizational culture and leadership* (4th ed.). San Francisco: Jossey Bass.

Schmoker, M. (2006). *Results now.* Alexandria, VA: Association for Supervision and Curriculum Development.

School Reform Initiative. (2012a). *Resource book.* Denver: CO: Author.

School Reform Initiative. (2012b). Retrieved from http://www.schoolreforminitiative.org

SEDL. (2011). Retrieved from http://www.sedl.org

Seidel, S. (1998). Wondering to be done: The collaborative assessment conference. In D. Allen (Ed.), *Assessing student learning: From grading to understanding* (pp. 21–39). New York: Teachers College Press.

Senge, P. (2006). *The fifth discipline: The art and practice of the learning organization.* New York: Random House.

Senge, P., McCabe, N., Lucas, T., Kleiner, A., Dutton, J., & Smith, B. (2000). *Schools that learn: A fifth discipline fieldbook for educators, parents, and everyone who cares about education.* New York: Doubleday.

Sergiovanni, T. S., & Starratt, R. J. (2002). *Supervision: A redefinition* (7th ed.). New York: McGraw-Hill.

Setting Norms for Collaborative Work. (n.d.). Retrieved from http://www.scoe.org/files/setting-norms.pdf

Singleton, G. (2011). Courageous conversations about race: An online course for achieving equity in schools. Retrieved from http://www.corwin-sinet.com/courses/glenn-singleton/Online course

Singleton, G., & Linton, C. (2006). *Courageous conversations about race: A field guide for achieving equity in schools.* Thousand Oaks, CA: Corwin Press.

Singleton, G., & Linton, C. (2007). *Facilitator's guide to courageous conversations about race.* Thousand Oaks, CA: Corwin Press.

Solution Tree. (2011). Retrieved from http://wwww.solution-tree.com

Spillane, J. (2005). *Distributed leadership.* San Francisco: Jossey Bass.

Stoll, L., & Louis, K. S. (2007). *Professional learning communities: Divergence, depth and dilemmas.* Berkshire, England: Open University Press.

Teachers College Reading and Writing Project. (2011). Retrieved from http:// tc.readingandwritingproject.com/

Teitel, L. (2006). *Supporting school system leaders: The state of effective training programs for school superintendents.* New York: Wallace Foundation.

Thompson-Grove, G. (2008). Foreword. In N. Dana & D. Yendol-Hoppey (Eds.), *The reflective educator's guide to classroom research: Learning to teach and teaching to learn through practitioner inquiry* (2nd ed.). Thousand Oaks, CA: Corwin Press.

Thompson-Grove, G. (n.d.). *Connections.* Retrieved from http://schoolreforminitia tive.org/protocol/doc/connections.pdf

Thompson-Grove, G., Evans, P., & Dunne, F. (n.d.). *Consultancy* protocol. Retrieved from http://schoolreforminitiative.org/protocol/doc/consultancy.pdf

Tuning Protocol. (n.d.). Retrieved from http://schoolreforminitiative.org/protocol/ doc/tuning.pdf

Wagner, T. (2004). The challenge of change leadership. *Education Week, 24*(99), 40–41.

Wagner, T., & Kegan, R. (2006). *Change leadership: A practical guide to transforming our schools.* San Francisco: Jossey Bass.

Waters, T., & Cameron, G. (2007). *The balanced leadership framework: Connecting vision with action.* Denver, CO: MCREL.

Weinbaum, A., Allen, D., Blythe, T., Simon, K., Seidel, S., & Rubin, C. (2004). *Teaching as inquiry: Asking hard questions to improve practice and student achievement.* New York: Teachers College Press.

Wentworth, M. (n.d.). Forming ground rules. Retrieved from http://schoolreformini tiative.org/protocol/doc/forming_ground_rules.pdf

What Kids Can Do, Inc. (2011). Retrieved from http://www.whatkidscando.org/

Zepeda, S., & Kruskamp, B. (2007). High school department chairs: Perspectives on instructional supervision. *High School Journal, 90*(4), 44–54.

Index

Note: An "f" with a page number denotes a figure; a "t" denotes a table.

About the Authors

Angela Breidenstein teaches in the Master of Arts in Teaching program at Trinity University in San Antonio, Texas, where she is an associate professor in the Department of Education. She directs the high school teacher preparation program and works with two professional development schools to support the learning of the schools, their students, the teachers, and the interns in teaching. She also has taught middle and high school German and social studies.

Kevin Fahey is the coordinator of programs in Educational Leadership at Salem State University in Salem, Massachusetts. In this role, he prepares school leaders to use the tools of critical friendship, facilitative leadership, and equitable practice to lead student, adult, and organizational learning. He also spent 25 years as a middle school teacher, high school department chair, district curriculum director, and elementary school principal.

Carl Glickman is president of the Institute for Schools, Education, and Democracy and professor emeritus of education at the University of Georgia. He began his career as a Teacher Corp intern in the rural south and later was a principal of award-winning schools in New Hampshire. At the University of Georgia he and colleagues founded the Georgia League of Professional Schools, a nationally validated network of high-functioning public schools dedicated to the principles of democratic education. He is the author or editor of 14 books on school leadership, educational renewal, and the moral imperative of education.

Frances Hensley is a founding member and director of the School Reform Initiative, a national organization that supports and promotes the learning of educators in transformational learning communities. She leads professional development in support of adult collaboration in schools and districts across the country and in international settings. For more than 20 years, she was a faculty member in the College of Education at the University of Georgia where she led K–12 school–university partnerships. She began her career as a special education teacher in rural north Georgia.